D1214163

THE PASSING SCENE

THE PASSING SCENE

A Commentary on Public Affairs

by

Charles P. Messick

UNIVERSITY OF DELAWARE

NEWARK, DELAWARE

DEDICATED TO THOSE WHO ADMINISTER
OUR GOVERNMENTS, LARGE AND SMALL

Printed in the United States of America

Contents

One Man's Life - An Introduction

I have been so bold as to undertake the writing of this book during a time for reflection — in America's bicentennial year — at what is generally regarded as a very advanced age. Having been born in 1882, I now look back on a life spanning almost half of our national existence. My health is still good, my mind active, and my memory full. But this is not an autobiography, nor is it a collection of reminiscences. It consists, rather, of reflections from my past and present, which — taken together — comprise one man's commentary on public affairs and is as much prospective as it is retrospective.

Age alone does not confer on one a license to write for the edification or guidance of others, and in any event I would not arrogate the right to tell others how to live. But the many years of my working life have been uniquely varied and public, including banking, farming, insurance, education, and government. And I have formed opinions, rightly or wrongly, of various degrees of firmness on many subjects, some of which I am motivated to share with others here. Some might say that this book represents my quest for immortality, but I would say that I neither seek nor expect fame in this or the next life, but rather I am motivated by much the same as I suppose motivates others to write books — by a creative impulse to communicate to others one's thoughts, worries, values, and sentiments about matters one considers important.

My principal interest has been and remains the administrative side of government, as I was a government employee in New Jersey for fifty years as a teacher and civil servant. And after "retirement" twenty-seven years ago, I became a consultant in both business and government, which obliged me to study public administration from both a civic and critical point of view, an indulgence I have never abandoned.

Accordingly, in these later years — as a retiree from the active scene — I yet study the administrative process and sometimes write my conclusions and suggestions for its improvement, hopefully for the advantage of the public and the more effective use of their tax dollar. I have written a book, *An Adventure in Public Personnel Administration*, published in 1973. I have coedited another, *The Principles of Public Personnel Administration*, from the unfinished manuscript of a deceased former associate, published in 1976. And during the past year I have written a number of articles on contemporary affairs that — together with a few of my earlier unpublished writings — form the substance of this present volume directed principally to those who must administer our governments large and small — from Washington through the states, counties, cities, towns and hamlets.

In my 1973 *Adventure* book I quoted John Stuart Mills' *On Liberty*, in which he said:

> The real advantage which truth has consists in this, that when an opinion is true it may be extinguished once, twice or many times but in the course of ages there will generally be found persons to rediscover it.

I repeat this quotation here because I believe it is an expression of great significance for any writing of serious intent, and because it serves to inspire me to set forth the "truth" — at least as I perceive it — in the following pages.

I harbor the hope that this little volume may help in some small measure to advance a more attentive and positive citizenship dedicated to the preservation of freedom.

Every period of our national history has been marked by problems or events that have endangered the freedom and opportunity guaranteed to us in America from its beginning. We call freedom our way of life. But over the years those freedoms have been eroded, and they no longer stand out so positively and clearly as once they did. Still, we are ahead of the rest of the world in maintaining these freedoms.

We should acknowledge the fact that these are difficult and dangerous days for our country, for all of us, individually and collectively. Yet, many of us go on our way with little thought and less action in changing or supporting the running of our great government, which yet remains the greatest government on earth.

We have been warned time and again in recent years, both inside government and outside, that public spending should be reduced and made more effective and that deficit spending must be discontinued. I dislike the person who says, "I told you so," but it needs to be said in repetition of that warning. I limit my expression of concern by suggesting that we should stop and look around and see what is happening and has been happening here in our country. We are the greatest nation on earth, but cannot be kept strong by division, by citizen neglect, and by indifference. It is, indeed, time for all our people to take stock, for we — the people — as citizens have made this government what it is and what it has become.

In speaking of our national flag, Woodrow Wilson once said:

> The things that the Flag stands for were created by the experiences of a great people. Everything it stands for was written by their lives. The Flag is the embodiment of history, not of sentiment. It represents the experience made by men and women — the experiences of those who do and live under that Flag.

I repeat — for it needs to be emphasized — it is time for all of us to stop, look, and listen, so that OUR FLAG shall continue to wave proudly over the ramparts of our freedom.

As a young teacher, with little training in the ways and methods of teaching, I soon discovered that to teach any subject one must be the master of that subject in the grade at least in which the teaching is being done. As I advanced in the profession, I found that the same principle prevailed in every activity and effort. I had looked forward to the time when I could speak convincingly, and write well enough, to be accepted. It follows that these accomplishments mean work, hard work. Edison, whose many inventions were vital to our success and for the world, once said he had never discovered anything by accident worth remembering. Devotion and dedication are the keys to success.

I have talked to all kinds of audiences, large and small, on many kinds of subjects, including audiences in ten or more of our great colleges and universities. I claim no success, but one thing I know that the speaker must possess. He must know what he is talking about. The same principle applies with equal force in writing. I say from my own experience that hard work is more dependable than inspiration, valuable as that may be, and knowledge is more dependable than hope, as essential as that may be.

This series of writings does not deal with any one subject, but they may be said, if one is not too critical, to have some relation to each other. They are, at least, my comments on the passing scene.

Rehoboth, Delaware
September 1976

CHAPTER 1

Politics and Politicians

Government is not limited in its responsibilities to being a public institution that collects our taxes nor to being the organization that directs our public affairs. Government does not give us funds for our support, but it does contribute to many of us who are in need, for educational purposes, and for a host of other purposes we as a people consider essential. Government is, to some extent, "political" — a characteristic that is always present even in what we regard as good government. It has been said recently that politics and politicians comprise the bridge that crosses the divide between the people and their government.

We have had chief executives who have ignored this relationship and have failed to win the confidence and trust of the people. Despite the fact that they were honest and devoted, they nevertheless failed.

President Hoover was a great engineer, and in terms of his background was perhaps the best qualified for the almost impossible job of the presidency. He attempted to stand with Washington and Lincoln, but he failed. He did not know how to gain the support of the people.

In terms of his background, on the other hand, President Truman was among the least qualified to comprehend and administer the duties of this great nation. But he was from the people, understood them, and talked their language. He was and remains one of our great presidents.

Franklin Roosevelt was not, to many people at least, a good executive or administrator. But in a crisis, he appealed to the people to help one another. He faced up to a great and imperative need, and the people understood and followed him. He led us out of that crisis — the Great Depression — but in doing so he taught us how to spend more public money than we took in. And we have become a nation of spendthrifts in practically all of our governments, big and little.

After years of warning, today we are trying — albeit too feebly — to stop this dangerous trend. The President demands a balanced budget. The Congress in effect says: "Yes, but let us overspend once more, even though we must ask our grandchildren to pay the bill." And there is the rub! Although the people of this country appreciate the difficulties, they want a balanced budget. But the best of us want to put it off for another year or two. It is the easy way. We have not the internal strength to act — knowledge, warnings and cold facts notwithstanding.

Thomas Jefferson once wrote:

> I place economy among the first and important virtues and public debt as the greatest danger to be feared, to preserve our independence. If we do run into such debt, we must be taxed on our meat and drink and our necessities and our comforts, in our labor and amusements. If we can prevent the government from wasting the labor of the people, under the pretense of caring for them, they will be happy.

When Benjamin Franklin cast his vote with the majority of the Continental Congress creating our national government, he observed: "Now you have a government if you can keep it." He meant that the government could be destroyed from the inside, but there was little danger of its destruction from the outside. George Washington cautioned:

> Do not suffer your good nature to say yes when you should say no. Remember it is the public not a private course that is to be benefitted or injured by your choice.

Dozens, even hundreds, of such warnings have been made through the years. We know, but we will not listen. Throughout our nation's history, we have been plagued with this wrong of overspending; yet we continue to travel the same road. The way is easy, but the end is dangerous and destructive.

In its March 8, 1976 issue, *U.S. News and World Report* asked this fearful but timely question: "Is Democracy Dying?" In the pages of that issue, eight prominent scholars from our great universities attempted to answer this question. Their answers were not reassuring, but there was some consensus that our politics have failed and that our politicians are the real culprits who have failed us. But in a larger sense, we — the body politic — have failed.

We need politicians, of course, but of the right kind. The dictionary definition of the term "politician" is one who has wisdom, who is prudent, diplomatic, and honest. But another meaning of the term is one who is skilled in being crafty, unscrupulous, selfish, and dishonest. My point is that the term "politician" is not necessarily negative, nor is it evil in itself. To me, a politician is one who has concern about his government and the state of its politics, and who is engaged in taking sides in political matters in the context of political parties. And political parties are not evil in themselves. They comprise the bridge that crosses the gap between politicians and government.

It is the abuse of these terms and the actions thereunder that makes them evil and dangerous. The real danger consists of dishonesty, even criminal activity, under the name of politics by politicians who seek personal power and profit regardless of the cost or damage to the integrity or trustworthiness of their government. We must admit that such corruption is rampant in our land. Venal politicians have destroyed governments in other lands and have significantly damaged governments here at home.

The day is far spent for us, and time is running out. We are already far along the road leading away from the land of the free and the home of the brave. There must be a reversal in the administration of our governments. We can do nothing more important in this bicentennial year than to move vigorously, with determination and without delay, in bringing this country back to the principles upon which it was founded — the principles of honesty, devotion, and patriotism in ourselves and in our governments.

CHAPTER 2

Education and Educators

Mr. Brady, our previous speaker, states again our old conviction that education is a first essential in our democracy. I agree with that, but I cannot share the complete confidence that he seems to express: namely, that things are generally right in our educational world, that we can meet our educational problems in these new days by an extension of our old educational philosophy and practice, and that we may well leave the whole matter to the educators.

My own doubts and reservations do not come by reason of lack of interest in our educational problems, nor from lack of appreciation of the contributions of education to American progress, nor from lack of confidence in the capacity and devotion of the great body of our teachers and leaders of educational thought and action. These doubts and reservations come to the fore when I see so much apparently lacking in the educational equipment of the young men and women pouring out of our schools and colleges, when I consider the threatening social and economic problems with which we are surrounded, and when I

AUTHOR'S NOTE: I gave the following address August 4, 1938 at a Conference for School Board Members and School Administrators, at Teachers College, Columbia University, in my capacity at that time as President of the Board of Education of Trenton, New Jersey.

note the attitudes of so many people toward the fundamental problems of life. They persist when I am compelled to acknowledge that we, through our educational system or otherwise, have not produced in the rank and file of our citizenship, in these products of our educational system, that sense of responsible citizenship and that active, persistent interest in public affairs that we have loudly proclaimed as a first essential in democratic government.

I express these doubts as one vitally interested in improving and adjusting our system of public education to our present-day needs, and out of a background that compels devotion to that system. I happen to be a product of the little red schoolhouse on the hill, which, incidentally, was not red and not on the hill. It was, however, the only avenue of educational opportunity open to me and to many other American children of school age forty to fifty years ago. I went from one district school as a pupil to another as a teacher; so did my brother and eight sisters. While I believe profoundly in public education, I think that we must look at our educational problems with open eyes, with a realism that will permit us to acknowledge what we see, and that we must measure and remeasure the results of our public education as they appear in our community and in our national life.

This conference in itself is indicative of the fact that we are not sure of the complete effectiveness of our educational undertakings. If we were, it would have a different theme. It may be true that some communities have met and solved their problems of public education, but by far the greater number have not.

We need some of the faith and practice of our educational pioneers. We need the same devotion to the cause of free education for every American boy and girl given by laymen and educators alike in the days of our early development. We need the same industry and desire to learn that is now supposed to have been common to school children of past generations. We need the same insistence upon mastery of essentials which, we now assume, characterized that period. But there is overwhelming evidence all about us that we need a great deal more than these things in our public school system of today if we are to make a successful attempt to cope with the social and economic and industrial forces we face today.

It is trite to say that we live in a new and different world and that we are faced with complications and complexities that have no counterpart in conditions existing fifty or a hundred years ago. Yet, this is so. And this conference will make no constructive contributions if it merely takes satisfaction in history or in present practice. We shall do well, I think, to approach this problem in a critical but constructive way. We should try to determine what may be wrong in our educational system, what may be its weaknesses, where it does not seem to meet our needs, rather than to emphasize its accomplishments, its strengths and its successes. We shall not be able to write a new formula, of course, but out of our deliberations may come something that will throw some light on the situation.

I do not believe that we can meet our educational need or any major problem by attempting to separate it from the whole broad problem of social progress. I hesitate to agree that there is a youth problem, peculiar to this particular day, that can be separated out from our whole social fabric and given special and distinctive treatment. I know that it is the present tendency to make divisions in this way and to talk about the problems of each class or group of our population as if they were things apart. I doubt this method of attack. In our attempts at solution of one problem, we are as likely as not — more likely, I think — to create as great, if not greater, disturbances in another. We have solved none of them by this method thus far, but we have seen the rise of class consciousness, which we have generally maintained has no place in our kind of democracy. While education must have as its major interest the training of youth, that training is for life, and not for the period of youth alone. What we seek is the orderly and effective flow of youth into our social and economic life. The answer will not be found if it involves the crowding out of some other group to make way for the new. Our America cannot afford to have "disillusioned youth," as Mr. Brady puts it; neither can it look with complacency upon "disillusioned" industrial workers, "disillusioned" farmers, "disillusioned" old age, or "disillusioned" employees. We stand or fall as a whole people, as a social and economic entity, and it is our job as citizens to seek the solution of the whole problem.

I recognize, of course, in the exploration of a question of this kind, how difficult it is to get down to cases. That difficulty is indicated, I think, in Mr. Brady's excellent paper. But just what are the specific answers to this question: "What education does my community desire?" What kind of education ought we to make available for American youth? We must, as he says, "bridge the ever-widening gap between the elementary school and the entry of youth into productive employment," but just how are we to do it? We must "continue the erection of school buildings," but buildings, alone, are not the answer. We must "devise . . . . knowledge essential for critical thinking," extend "appreciation of the responsibilities of citizenship," "take care that youth receives its rightful heritage of the traditions and ideals of our democracy and of the knowledge, the skill, the arts and sciences of the ages." We should provide a "full measure of intellectual development and spiritual growth." These are our general objectives, but so long as we citizens speak in general terms alone, we are not giving the kind of help to our educators that they need and want.

I cannot write the formula, of course. No person can do that. When it is written, it will be a composite product. But when I was asked to take this assignment, I wanted to know how the fathers and mothers, the professional men and businessmen of my own city, would answer this question. So I asked a number of them. Each of them labors under the same difficulty as Mr. Brady and I. Each is thinking in terms of his own particular interest. Each answered in a general way.

The public official, troubled about the tax rate and unemployment, says: "We are doing too much training for the professions, already overcrowded . . . . We are training great numbers . . . . with little or no thought of what place they will be able to fill in society . . . . Our training should be directed toward the development of those qualities of the individual that will make of him a man useful to himself and the community. Our educational plan must be kept within our ability to pay."

The industrialist says: "There are greater opportunities and greater demands for mechanics and skilled labor than in any other field of employment . . . . Greater emphasis should be put upon shop and factory work."

The professional engineer says: "Provide for varying intelligences; practical and trade courses for the less intelligent, but do not average down the intellectually superior."

The minister says: "Develop personality and train for Christian character."

The businessman says: "Vocational guidance and the responsibilities of citizenship are first essentials."

The doctor says: "Prepare school children for life as their industry and perseverance warrant."

The mother and clubwoman says: "Provide that education which will fit the greatest number for the normal responsibility of life and the exercise of their duties as citizens."

The parent-teacher leader pleads for a better elementary education where "the future doctor, bank president, and bricklayer learn together to read, write and figure . . . . that we may turn out a better generation, better informed, better adjusted, better trained, to solve the problems at which we, ourselves, have so far failed."

The fact of the matter is that none of us knows surely what subject matter, what practical arts, what cultural training, what health and recreational activities, what training for character and citizenship should go into our public school curricula. We do not know how these should be balanced and the best methods by which they may be made into the educational equipment of youth. There is no particular cause for discouragement in this situation, since to know these things would be to know the certain and valid answers to some of the most vital problems of our civilization. But there is ample cause for a healthy impatience at our failure to have developed and applied a system of public education that would more nearly meet our needs in these modern days.

The question of the cost of public education has been discussed earlier in this program, and I shall not attempt to add to that discussion. Those of us who sit on boards of education and who must plead for adequate school budgets year after year cannot forget, however, that there is a cost problem involved. I do not think that we have always gotten all of the returns in the way of educational improvements for which the people have paid. In the field of education, as in other public fields, we have spent too much for some things and too little for others. I am satisfied, however, that this democracy of ours can afford all of the education that it needs and requires and that should be paid for out of the public treasury.

It is highly important that we get together a working, tolerant, understanding combination of our educators and citizens representative of the whole range of our important interests, that we decide upon what education we require and must have, and that we develop within those determined limits the kind of curricula and instruction that we are calculated to best provide. I am satisfied that this can be done, but we cannot do it if the "doctors" insist that they, alone, shall diagnose the case and prescribe the whole treatment. We cannot accomplish it if citizens merely complain of the results of our educational system. We can make satisfactory progress only by a generous and complete area of cooperation and understanding between the professionals and citizens. That cooperation and understanding ought to be more articulate, more aggressive and more persistent than any efforts that have been made in this direction heretofore.

In our Trenton school system, we see the answer to the question, "What education does my community desire?" as involving and embracing these things:

1. Drill in, and reasonable mastery of, the three "R" fundamentals by all normal children.
2. Education for abnormal children, with opportunity for rapid advancement and additional training for the mentally superior, education geared to the slower pace and of a practical character for those below normal mentality; education adjusted to the needs and capacities of the children who are orthopedically handicapped, blind, or hard of hearing.
3. College preparation. One hundred seventy-five to two hundred members of our high school graduating classes enter

institutions of higher learning each year. It is essential, therefore, that we provide the necessary preparatory training.

4. Commercial training. Ours is an industrial community; our citizens find employment in considerable numbers in both the New York and Philadelphia metropolitan areas. We aim to provide, therefore, what is now regarded as adequate and appropriate high school commercial training.

5. Industrial preparation. Our school children, like those of practically all other communities, are attracted by the professions and the white-collar commercial jobs rather than those in the shop. We see the need for extended and improved shop courses, designed to provide basic training for those who enter the productive and service industries of the community. This part of our school activities has heretofore provided an outlet for those who must be trained manually. It is our notion that many more of those who are attracted to the cultural and commercial courses should be included in these more practical courses. There is not the overcrowding in the skilled and semiskilled trades and service industries. There is even a promised shortage. We think we shall do well to emphasize this type of training.

6. Health education. The same necessities for an adequate and intelligent health education exist with us as in every community. We seek to provide reasonable yet adequate training of this type.

7. Citizenship. No one can determine, perhaps, what adequate and effective training for citizenship really is. We are not content with theory alone. We seek to gear training to the everyday business of being a good citizen. We want our high school graduates to have a working knowledge of the operations of our local, state and national government and an intelligent interest in the news of governmental happenings, in the editorial comments, and in the significant interpretations of these happenings. We want them to under-

stand the place of semipublic, civic and social agencies in the community, the services that these agencies render, and citizen obligations and participation therein. We hope to develop habits of good citizenship, respect for public property, and a responsible sense of decent public behavior. In short, we hope that our combined training will make for active, intelligent, responsible citizenship.

8. Music and fine arts. We believe that these have a place in our public educational system, and we are willing to spend reasonable amounts to provide appreciation and understanding of these things that go far toward making the complete citizen.

9. Finally, we believe that adult education must now be recognized as part of our system of public education. We have done some of this heretofore. We are installing in this school year wider opportunities for adult education both in credit and noncredit courses, designed to add to intelligent citizenship, provide for leisure hours, and contribute to the retraining of those who seek this help.

These are objectives, and I apologize for my inability to state precisely how to reach them. In summary, it can be said that education is our most important business. Each one of us, and not just the professionals, must be responsible for its advancement. It is essential to our democracy.

CHAPTER 3

Teaching and Teachers

The foregoing address was given thirty-eight years ago and at that time it was reasonable to expect that by this second centennial year of nineteen hundred and seventy-six, we would have made vast improvements in our educational progress and problems that were then troubling us. The truth of the matter is that the differences that troubled us then have grown greater. They have reached into our colleges and institutions. Our public schools are centers of rebellious students, striking teachers, and reduced educational standards; police walk the grounds and buildings to protect students from each other and teachers from the pupils. The costs of our educational system have continued to rise.

The purpose of that 1938 meeting was for a general discussion of our school problems, and representatives of school boards were invited in the hope that they would return to their homes with a better understanding of the problems of the teachers and would be more active in their support. The school administrators discussed their own problems earnestly and at some length. Their position was that they had developed their plans and procedures. They believed they were right and they asked for the support of the school boards and the people. In short, they asked for no interference; they wanted to handle their own business in their own way.

Speaking for the boards and, as I hoped, for the fathers and mothers of the children, I tried to emphasize the fact that I was not finding fault with our teachers or with their methods, that I had been a teacher myself, but they were teaching our children. The parents wanted to know something of current teaching methods. We, board members, were their representatives, and it was our duty to keep informed as to the quality of our educational systems, to make constructive suggestions, if we believed that we could do so constructively, when and as we thought it necessary. It may have been that the teachers accepted our suggestions with some reservations and some doubt. I believe that the meeting continued with good feeling and was profitable to both the administrators and the school board representatives.

Many years have passed since that meeting. Great changes have been made in our way of life. The little red schoolhouse is no more. We have built mansions for our schools. We have equipped them with everything our teachers have wanted. We have shortened the school day. We have reduced the size of classes. We have tried to keep the teachers' pay within the level of that of the community. With all of this there is no peace in our schools, or anywhere in our land, for that matter. Where there should be cooperation, there is conflict. Where there should be respect and order in the class room, there is bedlam. Peace officers patrol the school grounds and walk the halls to protect both the teachers and the children, and the end is not yet.

There are of course many devoted teachers in our schools. Teaching is a noble profession and worthy of the pride of every teacher. Unfortunately this is not the case. The great teacher organizations have recognized their strength. They seek power. They have that now, but they want more and are getting it. They no longer ask; they demand. They no longer confer on terms and arrangements; they make them. Most unfortunately they thrive on disorder, and they add to it by pickets and by strikes. It has been reported in the news media that our teacher organizations now propose to join other organized groups in the building of one great organization under one leadership. Should that plan be consummated, it could, at will, bring the machinery of industry and government to a grinding stop. The result of such a catastrophe is beyond contemplation.

I was born in the back country when opportunity for schooling beyond reading and writing and arithmetic was hard to come by. We were a family of ten children, and we went down the lane to the little one-room school. Our teachers had received their education in similar schools, passed the required tests — which were limited and elementary at best — were certified by the County Superintendent, and went out to teach in other such schools scattered over the county and state. My brother and I and our eight sisters all followed the same road as we and they reached the required age, took and passed the tests, and received our certificates. We were a family of teachers. Two of our younger generation are teachers now.

I wanted to go to college. I taught in my one-room school for four years and, by home study and reading, struggled to span the bridge from a poorly prepared farm boy to college entrance. In my long experience out in the world I have carried the memories of the devoted teachers — working for a pittance — and, later, the kindly professors, who helped me along the way. I came to look upon teachers as special people and teaching as something apart from other callings and professions. And there is ample cause for that special devotion and dedication in the teacher, for both he and she have the fearful responsibility of building character and shaping the minds of coming citizens in this troubled world. He or she is the ideal of the young child and the model for the older ones.

But education alone does not make a teacher. There are character and convictions involved. The teacher must know this country, its history and for what it stands, and of the long struggle of mankind from the cavern to the Crown, to the Cross, to America. He or she is free, with a duty to teach change in a changing world to meet the changing needs of the people and the way by which changes may be brought about. He or she is not entitled to teach contempt for government and rebellion against it. He or she are yet free agents in America and if they believe that to bring about radical change is their mission, they have the privilege of saying so — but not in the classroom. We have great teachers in America — we need more!

We need good teachers, dedicated teachers. William Lyon Phelps, one of our great teachers at the university level, once said:

> I had rather earn my living by teaching than in any other way. In my mind, teaching is not merely a life work, a profession, an occupation, a struggle; it is a passion. I love to teach as a painter loves to paint, as a musician loves to play, as a singer loves to sing, as a strong man rejoices to run a race. Teaching is an art — an art so great and so difficult to master that a man or woman can spend a long life at it, without realizing much more than his limitations and his mistakes, and his distance from the ideal. But the main aim of my happy days has been to become a good teacher, just as every good architect wishes to be a good architect, and every professional poet strives toward perfection.

Great teachers are like that. This prattle about teachers and other public workers being deprived of rights that other citizens have is silly — a transparent screen to hide a feeling of guilt.

I have spent most of my life in the public service. I am not a second-class citizen. I have served the people of my state and nation; I am a privileged citizen. There is no higher service than that except serving the children, which is the teacher's task. I have always felt more at home with teachers of every class and at every level than those of any other calling. I am, and have been, a friend of teachers, as one of them, as a citizen, and as a long-time member and sometimes president of my city board of education; I have wanted for them adequate pay, tenure as long as they render worthy service, pensions, considerate treatment, satisfying careers, and opportunity for advancement as their talent and as opportunity offers. Teachers have all these advantages in our country now. They need, too, the understanding and respect of parents and the public. These things they must earn for themselves.

Somewhere in the long past I read or heard a story of a teacher who had gone through one of those difficult experiences that comes to all teachers. She had had a bad day. The school room was as dreary as the weather outside. The children were restless, they seemed to have lost interest in their studies, their lessons were poorly prepared and, in spite of everything she tried to do, she could not get any response from them. When the school day ended and the children were dismissed — with an outlook as dark as the day outside — she sat, with her hands pressed against her throbbing temples, thinking of her difficulties and wondering if she had not made a mistake in trying to be a teacher and whether she should not give it up altogether. And as she sat in a half daze or half dreaming, suddenly the little school room became a great auditorium filled with people. The children she had just dismissed were there. The men and women of years ago with greying hair and wrinkled brows — signs of life's cares and struggles — were there. All of those she had taught appeared — the successful ones, the failures, all. And there was great babel of voices — everybody talking to their friends and neighbors, and as she came awake the picture changed as suddenly as it had come into her vision. She was back in her little school room, but in that change she saw all of the great assembly pointing a finger at her and she heard them say in a voice hinting of accusation and pleading as well, "Remember! It is we you teach." It would be a most helpful incident if our teachers could hear that cry again.

CHAPTER 4

Strikes and Strikers

The following will be accepted by some people as a recognition of a serious situation in the passing scene in American life and by others as a development necessary for the protection of the presumed rights and interests of labor. The facts are that we have strikes, that they must be dealt with, that they enter into the relationships between the employer and employee, and that they vitally affect employees in the public service and politics.

I have always said that I would not strike against my government. I accepted public employment as a matter of choice. I accepted the responsibilities that were involved in that acceptance. I had the right to leave that employment, if a situation affecting me or my service could not be adjusted to my satisfaction. As long as I was holding to that employment, I had no right to withhold my services or strike. I look upon the rights of all public workers in this way. I was a charter member of my state public employees association. I yet carry my membership card. I believe in such associate grouping of civil servants but not for the purpose of withholding their services or in striking. Notwithstanding the brave and beautiful words of Thomas Jefferson — that all men have inalienable rights to life, liberty and the pursuit of happiness — these rights are neither God-given nor inalienable. The words are beautiful rhetoric. They have always been touted as something for all to cling to, but the hard facts are that we the people have no rights except those that are given to us by the country or society in which we live. It is true that our society has given us more individual freedom and more rights and privileges than have been provided by any other nation. I want to keep it that way. But history tells me that any nation that cannot or does not enforce its own laws and its regulations thereunder does not long survive. I want my country to endure.

Yet strikes are the order of the day throughout our whole economy, and teachers now lead the way. They flaunt the laws. They ignore the dangers to the public welfare. They strike over little as well as big things. They strike against adding fifteen minutes to their workday and the adding of two or three additional members to their classes when there is nowhere else to send them. Some spokesmen for teachers say they strike for the sake of the children. A teacher who has merely a job may say that; a teacher who sees teaching as a service of devotion will not.

There was a time in the long past that the man who worked with his hands, the laborer, was oppressed. He was hired and fired by employers without prior notice and left to his own devices and efforts to get along and provide for his family. Employers must share the responsibility for these conditions. They hastened the labor-employer conflicts that have become a part of our way of life, as our industrial system expanded and we came into the assembly line type of employment and the work of the man who worked with his hands became narrow and specialized. He could do well his own job but was unfamiliar with that of his fellow worker down the line. He became classified. Situations such as these brought the workers into groups, the advance guard of unions. Unions brought power, and so the unions are dominant today. Power carefully used brings safety but used recklessly destroys. We are not a perfect society, so the power of labor can and does bring misery and need to many while it brings comfort and assurance to a few.

I have spent most of my working life in the public service. During that service I gained substantial recognition throughout America in the development of the principles of personnel management in government. I would be less than honest if I said I believed that unions should be recognized in that service with all of the rights and procedures they exercise in our great industrial system. Boards, commissions and executives give in, pay the price, and forgive the offenders their challenges. There is a limit to this procedure. We are beginning to believe that that limit has been reached and must be recognized. Labor has an important part in the functioning of the machinery and business of private and public enterprise; it can destroy both if we here and others in the world follow this course. It may be added that other nations, even new nations, are apt students.

I am not against associations, groups or unions as a part of our body politic; I was a charter member of an association of public employees in New Jersey where I spent almost all the years of my working life. I still carry my association card, but I have said many times with some risk, I would not strike against my government. I still believe that. I am convinced that I am right. I recognize, of course, that strikes and strikers are with us in our public and private life. I know that they have become a part of our public life. I know too that they must be dealt with. I do not exempt industry and government from blame. In the long or short run, the people pay. I do not believe that committees, executives or any authority can bargain away public funds that have not yet been appropriated. I do not believe that employees can ignore and disobey judicial orders and decisions. I repeat that government must be master in its own house.

Looking back over the long years of my experience, I remember Coxey's Army, and its effort to walk to Washington. I heard Samuel Gompers speak to a legislative assembly, and he asked for fair and reasonable relationships among business and government and labor. I knew Luther Steward who organized the employees in the Post Office division in Washington. I knew Arnold Yerkes as a friend for many years who first talked about the unionization of public employees. And none of these leaders said anything about the right of public employees to strike. I remember a long and serious discussion with Mr. Yerkes about this. I expressed my fear to him that there would come a time when labor leaders would make no exception of public employees with regard to striking. I very greatly regret that my forecast was accurate. One has to but look around and see what is going on. A dozen states, scores, perhaps hundreds, of counties, towns and districts that are sustained by public money are having strikes, and to my great regret, teachers lead the procession.

It is proper and desirable for public employees and teachers to join associations and groups kindred to their own interests. I do not believe that any public employee should strike. And teachers should not strike under any circumstances. But with their new-found liberties, they do so and are more exacting in their demands. The teacher who strikes destroys his usefulness by that act. As individuals, teachers must teach to their children respect for their country, their government and its institutions, the necessity for law and order and the responsibilities of citizenship. The true teacher is a dedicated citizen. He is in the business of training for citizenship. He must set an example. He cannot take any other attitude and yet be a teacher. If he does he is in the wrong profession.

The public employee must and is expected to be a good and honorable servant of the public and obedient to the governing laws. Calvin Coolidge put the matter tersely and in a few words when he said that no employee could strike against his government when the police force struck in Boston. I know the story that some one of his associates when he was governor of Massachusetts said that for him, and when he found that it was popular he let it stand. It matters not who said it, it was sound statesmanship. The approval of the people of the nation was shown by choosing him as vice-president and president in later years.

We would be a stronger and better nation if there were no strikes, but we have them. There must be found a better way to settle our political and class differences. There must be imposed upon those who violate the laws the penalty that the laws prescribe. Forgiveness of one law dulls another law. Unfortunately the flaunting of one statute does not bring respect for observance of another. The common truth is that in his workmanship, the worker — professional, tradesman, or laborer — whenever he works must give enough of value in his service as the product of that service is worth in the common market.

CHAPTER 5

Rebellion

From the foregoing, it follows that today the word is rebellion — rebellion against authority, rebellion by individuals against the "establishment," rebellion by organized groups against law and order, rebellion by children against their parents, rebellion by public employees against their government — rebellion everywhere, and seemingly at times, by everybody.

These attitudes are not only disconcerting; they are dangerous. Nevertheless, too many of us talk about them cautiously or not at all, hoping, I suppose, that they will go away, but there is no indication that they will do so. I have no plan that is not open to others. I represent no one but myself, but I do have some convictions both about the position that government should take and that it and the people must take, relatively soon, if our own people through their governments are to keep and maintain order and safety.

The whole issue of rebellion versus public order resolves itself into a single sentence, expressed in these few words: Government must be master in its own house. As a master, it has many obligations. It must be just; it must be honest. It must be fair with its working forces. It must see to it that these forces are organized into working units, directed and supervised with concern, to the end that they may perform a fair day's work every working day — of work that needs to be done, and no other — that they are well paid at levels in the community for comparable service, that they shall have opportunity to look to satisfactory careers according to their capacity and devotion, and that they be given adequate retirement pay so they may live in quiet dignity when their work is done. A large contract one may say! It is, but the ends sought are as great as the responsibility involved.

These same requirements and obligations apply with equal force to all citizens individually, as groups, organized or unorganized.

Public employees are different from their fellow workers in private enterprise since they work directly for all of us, and — whether we like it or not — they are not as free as workers in private enterprise. The public employee must give up some of what he may call his rights. He may not withhold his work as he feels like it. He may not act as he pleases, nor do other things that public employees are forbidden to do. Public employees come into the service of their own free will. As a rule they now have permanence of pay and position greater than those of their fellow workers in private enterprise. They may leave or accept other jobs in or out of the service at will. But they are always on parade; that is to say, they are always under both public and private scrutiny. They should be, and are, expected to set higher standards than the average worker.

This indicated difference between the private and public worker does not set either apart in his status or his stature. There was a time when a laborer was considered a sort of chattel property to be worked hard, paid at low rates, and left to his own devices when he grew old or unable to work at his job or trade, but that time is long past. Employers have long since discovered that workers should be treated better as a matter of self interest. The thunder of bare feet — the rise of the workers in importance — has come of age. Unfortunately, at times workers are inclined to force improved working conditions — such as higher pay and what we call fringe benefits — through strikes, picketing and, too often, violence.

As for myself, I take it for granted that both public employees and those in private enterprise have a right, if they wish, to organize, to petition, and to urge consideration for the improvement of their working and pay conditions. I do not agree that they should, or have a right to, strike. For most of my working life I was a government employee and an official. I took the position of my own accord that I would not strike against my government. I want it to endure and "Government must be master in its own house." If it is not, it cannot long endure.

As I stated earlier, the early advocates of worker organizations did not propose strikes. Arnold Yerkes, Samuel Gompers, and Luther Steward had high motives and were not enemies of management. None mentioned strikes.

We have gone too far in America in compromising with rebellious attitudes. The time has come when we must face the facts and apply the remedies that our laws already provide. We have tried too long to compromise, to trade the public interest for domestic peace. Forgiveness has not worked; we are left with punishment of those who dangerously defy our government. There is in all of these conditions, however, some hopeful light. Labor through its leaders and employers is talking about the uselessness of strikes, that the interests of both as well as of all of us is the same. Understanding cooperation must come soon.

As I now have more freedom in the use of my time, I try not only to keep up with significant events but I read history. And from history I have come to a point where, like Poe's raven, I see or think I see something sitting at my chamber door. And I wonder about the life of governments. They come, they achieve power, they rule, they pass from history. Do nations, like people, grow old and die? If so, is there any relation to the length of their lives? In 1976, we celebrate the two-hundredth anniversary of our birth as a nation. We have achieved wealth and strength beyond that of any nation in the world's history. Are we getting old and losing the spirit, the determination, the unity that made us great? The trail of history is littered with the wrecks of empires all along the way, and none have held for two hundred years to the same tenets of faith, purpose, and authority under which they came into being. Where does our country stand in this picture? As we celebrate, are we together? Do we have the faith, the rugged determination that marked our building?

We are divided today as never before in our history, so far as our civil affairs are concerned. We are washing our dirty linen for all to see in a day in which the slogan is "The people have a right to know." We not only publish our own misdeeds at home but insist that the world shall know them and pass judgment. And the world looks on with amazement and disgust. Have we grown old? And what is ahead? It is time to think on these things.

CHAPTER 6

Perils of These Times

Some time ago I attended a conference of significance to many of us in the United States and to many in a number of other countries. In the many conference meetings, there was a spirit of peace, friendship and cooperation. As I mingled with that great body of men, I kept thinking about the purposes for which those there assembled came and about the refreshing atmosphere of kindness and understanding one could feel everywhere. I thought, too, of the contrast of this atmosphere with the conflicts of men throughout our own country and the nations of the world. Where there should be peace, there is war. Where there should be trust, there is doubt. Where there should be tolerance, there is intolerance. Where there should be justice, there is vengeance that too often marks our dealings with each other.

These are perilous times not only for our people, but for nations large and small. Every day the news media reports these differences, and agreements are as rare as the most sought-after antiques. We need only look around us to see these conflicts, and we must know that our own great country cannot survive, prosper, and assure freedom and opportunity to our people, if we permit dangerous and destructive disharmony to continue to prevail over harmony. There must be an awakening of the people of this nation, and as a matter of fact of the nations of the world, if we and they are to escape nuclear disaster. Time is running out. The day is far spent. The reckoning is drawing near.

Benjamin Franklin was a man of many talents but he was a statesman of rare ability. He understood that this young country would have to face difficulties almost impossible to overcome and would have to take risks seemingly almost certain of failure as it struggled for life and recognition with few friends among the nations of the world. Franklin foresaw many of our troubles. And we have had troubles that threatened national survival many times as we moved on toward strength and greatness. But we have surmounted them and maintained the concepts and standards with which we began. We are now in another of these testing times.

There was and is both beauty and resources in this land, beyond those of any other country. We have destroyed much of that beauty, with reckless disregard of its meaning and value, and we have destroyed much of these resources by our wasteful practices, but we have yet built the greatest country in the world with standards of living and wealth unequaled since the world began. But we have neglected the things that assure the endurance of men and nations. We are a divided people torn asunder by jealousy, hate, greed, and suspicion. Crime walks our streets, roads, and byways boldly and unafraid, defying our defensive forces, and destroying life and property. Our criminals go free or escape adequate punishment while, too often, we abandon the victims.

To convince ourselves, or to soothe our consciences, we call in the psychologists, the psychiatrists, and others skilled in the ways of lawbreakers to tell us the reasons why people commit crimes and aid our enemies. Whatever may be their knowledge beyond that of the rest of us, they do not reduce the crime and unrest that leads to these ends, that must be demanded by us — the people. And punishment to fit the crime must be meted out to the offenders, certain and sure. The peril grows as the days pass. The people wait on the decision.

CHAPTER 7

The Way to Good Government

The stated purposes of this Institute are the study and discussion of governmental problems, the consideration of the underlying economic and social conditions, and the advancement of popular understanding of current public questions. These are matters of vital and immediate public concern. Government as a whole, or in any of its parts, cannot be expected to adjust itself automatically to the rapidly changing conditions progress brings. We must consider seriously our social, economic and governmental problems and seek diligently the way for our continued development.

The emphasis that is to be placed upon the study of municipal and local government at this session is not, I take it, accidental, but deliberate. It is in recognition of the fact that government does not develop from the top, but from the people; that improvement in the processes of government is not first evident in the nation or in the state, but in the municipality; that public opinion and public understanding do not first find expression in a national movement, but in community effort;

AUTHOR'S NOTE: I include here extracted remarks from my address in 1931 at the Institute of Public Affairs of the University of Virginia because they appear to me to be as relevant today as they were 45 years ago.

and that we must look to the improvements, the undertakings and the experimentations in our local governments to give tone and character and direction to all government. Thirty years ago political scientists were deploring the failure of city government. It was rather widely agreed that municipal administration had broken down and that we must look to the state and the nation for leadership, for inspiration, and for protection against our own inability to administer community affairs. We now see more clearly that advances in the method and effectiveness of public administration originate and grow in local jurisdictions, that if cities cannot solve their own problems and govern themselves, the nation largely made up of urban communities will not be able to govern itself, and that as goes the municipality so goes the state and nation.

Adequate, economical and effective municipal administration involves many questions. Great improvements have come in the form of the administrative machinery, the centralization of responsibility and authority, and the demand for the specially trained public executive, as is illustrated in the city manager and comparable movements; but most students of government have made the common error, I think, of failing to give consistent thought and consideration to the personnel problem not only in municipal government but in all government. We have spent a great deal of thought and effort in designing and building our complicated governmental machine, but we have paid relatively little attention to the qualifications, the selection, the organization, the training and the supervision of the working crew.

Notwithstanding the "plan" infection that has spread over the country and the world, I offer no "plan" for the solution of our governmental problems. I have limited faith in government by time program or by any program that does not take into consideration the normal needs, interests, and desires of the people. There are no short cuts to good government. The processes of government are evolutionary, and no political poultices nor patented panaceas will prove effective. Good government depends not so much on the "Man on horseback" as upon the active and intelligent interest and participation of the citizenship of which it is composed. It is a hopeful sign, I think, that you should recognize in a public way and consider formally as a part of this big problem of municipal administration the matter of the public personnel and its relation to effective government.

In presenting this subject I realize that there is a great lack of accurate information and understanding of the real aims and purposes of modern personnel administration in the public service. I recognize the fixed prejudices and determined conclusions of many administrative officers and numerous citizens who have observed the limited success of some civil service systems. I recognize also that political scientists have devoted their energies to the theories of government rather than to its operation. More recently, however, they are turning to the more practical parts of public administration, including budgets and budgetary control, centralized purchasing, executive management, financial regulation, zoning, departmental organization, and the like. In the meantime this question of adequately handling the public personnel has persisted. It has grown in size, in cost and in importance. It can no longer be brushed aside or ignored. It cuts across and directly affects every other part and function of government, and some of those who have studied it most are convinced that it overshadows all other problems of good and effective public administration. I share that opinion. I do not mean to imply that form and orderly arrangement are not essential. I insist only that out of the study of the plan and the powers and procedure of government there has been developed more accurate knowledge than is now being used or that can be put into practical operation within the next twenty-five years. In our performance we have always lagged behind our knowledge. We need now to consolidate our gains rather than seek new discoveries. Most of all we need to come to some understanding about the human problems involved and how they may be met, what are the functions of the personnel agency in the public service and what are the relations of the proper discharge of these functions to good public administration.

In America we are inclined to measure the importance of any business or thing by its size and cost. Considered by these standards government takes first rank in all business, and personnel becomes the first question of government. It is variously estimated that government is costing in America one-sixth of our national income. The earnings of the American people in one day of each week go directly or indirectly to the support of public administration. Aside from our debt service, at least fifty per-cent of all public expenditures go into the public payroll. Government is continually undertaking new services, and the numbers of civil employees are persistently increasing.

But cost is not the only factor to be considered. There are the quality and quantity of work, the assurance that adequate service shall be rendered, honesty, integrity, the determination of the scope and character of the government, its policies, its ends and its proper functions. William Penn once said that "Governments like clocks take their movement from the direction that men give them." Government is no better and no worse than the officials and employees who do its work. They reflect the standards and desires of their employers, the people. They not only shape the policies and undertakings of government, but they exercise a powerful, even a governing, influence in determining how public money shall be spent. Governments and the individuals who serve them may be honest but they can hardly be effective, especially in populous areas, unless there is organization, regulation, supervision, and control of the public personnel. S. S. McClure, in addressing the School of Public Administration of the University of Southern California, has said that in his study of the governments of the world the successful ones are those that have trained the permanent employees and the failures are those that have not. "Democracy," he said, "is essentially the strongest form of government, yet the United States, which gave democracy to the world, is the only nation that refuses to benefit by it." The ablest and most effective civil servants are in those jurisdictions where there are organized personnel divisions and where they are most vigorously administered. The poorest quality of service is found in those jurisdictions that have not recognized the significance of the personnel problem of government and are still under dominant partisan control.

It is essential that the welfare and regulation of these millions of workers in government and the tremendous sums of money paid for personal service be given serious and adequate attention. It would be natural for local governments to look to the federal service for an adequate procedure for handling their personnel problems. The federal government had made some progress, as have a number of states, but it has not yet centralized its personnel control nor has it provided machinery and authority adequate for the effective handling of the greatest personnel problem of the world. It is not in criticism, but as a statement of fact, to say that the federal government does not lead but follows in progressive administration. Municipalities, for instance, set up budgets before they were common in state administration, and 46 of the 48 states had established budget systems before the federal government got around to this fundamental matter.

A few examples will illustrate the approach to the personnel problem that some of our progressive cities and counties and a few states are making. Even the smallest employer must make some arrangement for handling leaves of absence of various kinds. In the public service it is customary to allow a vacation with pay of two or three weeks each year and in some cases a month. In addition, by formal action, by practice, by custom or tradition, the employee who is sick is allowed to be absent with pay for periods ranging from a week to a month. The public employee not only theoretically but actually may be absent from his duty with pay throughout one month in twelve. This means that the public as an employer pays its workers something like a half billion dollars a year when they may be absent from their duties for vacation or on account of illness. Ordinary business prudence demands that when the welfare of millions of people is at stake and hundreds of millions of dollars are being spent, there should be a definite procedure governing vacations and leaves for the whole public service, and administrative machinery set up that will require general observance of that procedure. Progressive cities and counties and states are undertaking this sort of regulation. They want to assure themselves, first, that vacation and sick leave privileges are not abused; second, that vacation and sick leave policies as expressed in their established procedure are carried out; and, third, that the worthy public servant shall be fairly dealt with and that the public interest shall be conserved.

We must not forget that the service that government undertakes to render is dependent upon the quality and character of the work of the public employee. Public employees are not lazy and grasping. They may and do fail in many ways, but they are as loyal, as capable, and as amenable to discipline and supervision as are any other class or group. The weakness in public administration cannot fairly be placed upon the public employee, but rather upon the people who select or elect the administrative and policy-determining officers and upon those officers who are charged with the selection, the organization, the assignment, and the supervision of the working forces under their control. In one county jurisdiction where a two-week vacation with pay is prescribed, an actual recent count showed that 250 of the 1300 public employees declined to avail themselves of their vacation privileges. Some preferred to remain on the job in order to keep abreast of their daily work; others did not take their authorized vacation because they preferred to forego this privilege rather than to entrust their work to other hands. A single instance of this kind is not sufficient proof, of course, of the interest and industry of all public employees, but in many jurisdictions about which I have some personal knowledge, the same condition prevails.

Another interesting movement in those cities, counties and states that are giving most attention to their personnel problems is the measurement of performance on the job. All who have dealt with this question either in business or in industry realize the tremendous differences in the quantity and quality of work done by different employees in different kinds of jobs and the difficulty involved in establishing a system that will adequately and fairly measure the things that distinguish capable service from failure and productive employees from those who render less service than that for which they are paid. Experience shows that in a school system, for instance, the principal, the assistant superintendent and the superintendent regularly are unable to agree as to which is the best and which is the poorest teacher in a given school, and much less are they able to agree as to which of two teachers, nearly alike in performance, is really doing the best work.

Within the last three years, a measuring system has been devised by a public personnel administrator for measuring the performance of teachers, clerks, stenographers, inspectors, laborers and others, with a high degree of reliability and validity. As a consequence, a number of cities, counties and two or three states are already using this newly developed technical tool as a means of measuring the performance of their employees so as to act intelligently in granting or withholding promotion to higher positions, in making upward and downward adjustments in rates of pay, in determining the order of layoffs when forces must be reduced, in arriving at decisions as to employees laid off who are worthy of reemployment, and in discovering those who because of their inability to meet reasonable standards of performance would be transferred, demoted or separated from the service.

There are other parts of an adequate personnel administration in the public service. Existing positions must be classified as to their requirements, their duties and their responsibilities. The question of establishing new positions, and eliminating old positions no longer needed, must be given attention. Compensation schedules for every position in the service in keeping with the going rate of pay in business and commercial enterprise, the degree of the responsibility and duties carried, the possibilities of advancement and the social worth of the service must be determined. Adequate machinery is necessary for recruiting properly qualified persons who possess the industry, the integrity and the ability to render capable and acceptable service. Uniform and just procedure must be established for the regulation of employees in the service, designed to maintain their morale and their interest. Provision must be made for the separation of those who no longer merit employment, for the retirement and pension of those grown old in the service, and for proper disciplinary measures in cases of delinquency or violation of accepted standards of performance and conduct. Every problem and situation among all of the difficult and intricate relationships existing between the department head, the supervisory officer and the individual worker, between departments and divisions of government, together with the relationships between each individual employee and each department or division and of the government as a whole must be carefully determined and provided for.

I shall not undertake to exhaust the subject or to weary you with other illustrations of what high-grade personnel work as a part of public administration now means. No city, county or state is under any more obligation to have a personnel system of the 1910 type than it is, when it purchases an automobile, to buy one which represents the best 1910 model. The state of Maryland has a personnel system of recent model. The state of Virginia's personnel system corresponds to Mr. Ford's Model T. The federal government has made considerable advances in its personnel administration, but it has not succeeded by a long measure in bringing its model up to date. This is a matter of choice on the part of governments. If they desire they can advance their personnel systems to the 1931 model rather than the 1910 or 1915 or 1920, and I venture to say that within a quarter of a century, and probably within ten years, the voters and taxpayers in practically every public jurisdiction will be demanding and enjoying the benefits of the sort of personnel system of which, as yet, only a limited number of the more progressive have seen fit to avail themselves.

The same factors and considerations that determine success in other activities of government will bring success in the field of personnel control. Public personnel administration will be effective to the degree that it is recognized as a major function of government; that the correct organization, funds and support are provided; that the general public and their chosen administrators are convinced of the fact the workers are more important than the machine; and that they are willing to initiate and support the best demonstrated administrative procedure in the selection, regulation and control of the personnel in government.

Besides the federal government, 10 states, including several of the most populous, and some 300 cities, including every city of 250,000 and more population except only Indianapolis, and a limited number of counties and other local governments have some kind of a personnel system. If we include teachers, library workers, social workers and other professional classes, probably one-half of all government employees are selected with some attempt to establish and maintain minimum standards as to training and qualifications and with some prospect of permanent tenure. Only in a few jurisdictions, however, is there a well thought-out, comprehensive, and adequate program for central personnel control.

Effective personnel administration cannot be accomplished merely by good intentions only, or by fervid oratory, but by the determined application of those principles and policies that have been tested and proved to be sound. America has come far along the road to adequate self-government, but we cannot afford to forget that our experiment in democracy is not complete. A modern philosopher said a week or two ago that if the books were closed today and the debits and credits cast up we must be recorded as having failed and that America would go down in history as having been strangled by her own successes. I am inclined to think, indeed it is my conviction, that a further advance in good government in America lies in the improvement of the organization, the recruiting, the regulation and the handling of the personnel rather than in the establishment of administrative codes, the writing of new charters or the devising of new machinery for public administration. Whether it be measured in terms of costs, in numbers, in quality or in its relation to better government, the effective handling of the public personnel remains the most important, unsolved problem in the whole field of government.

CHAPTER 8

Sixty Years of Public Personnel Management

I am pleased that you have invited me to speak to this group of former and present officeholders in this organization. In 1906 we were organized as the Civil Service Assembly. I was then entering the Senior Class in Delaware College. That organization was small in numbers, weak in standing, uncertain of the future, without plan or program, but it stayed alive.

Today, in 1966, is your birthday, and business and professional organizations use their anniversary days as the time to look over their present situation, to consider the place from which they have come and lay out their plans for the future. In these sixty years you have made progress. You have gained strength, reputation and influence, but you have not completed your journey. You have a long way to go; in fact you will never come to the end of the line for it is always ahead. An organization dealing with people, their lives and relationships will not find any convenient resting place. If it stops, it dies. The problems

---

AUTHOR'S NOTE: I gave the following address in 1966 on the 60th anniversary date of the Public Personnel Association to its then current and former officeholders. Founded in 1906 as the Civil Service Assembly, I served as president of the Association in 1922 and 1930-33. Since 1973, the Association has been known as the International Personnel Management Association.

and that road ahead are today your first considerations — your most important business.

As you pause in your deliberations to do honor to Ken Warner, who is laying down the burden of directing your work for the twenty years past, and to name his successor, you must of necessity consider your program for the future.

In those considerations that are affected in many ways by your past, you will run into the names and work of two men named Messick and Telford. I am the creator of this secretariat, and Fred Telford was my first mate. We are here today to testify to our continuing interest in what you have done, what you have accomplished up to this time, and we hope to be of some help to you in planning your future. Incidentally we are here to show you how we look after thirty years of struggle in this work and an indication of how you may look after thirty years of effort in this business of personnel management.

Ken Warner has earned your respect and commendation. He has advanced in many substantial ways the project of the personnel of government and its effective administration. I have talked with him from time to time over the years and he has been generous enough to say that I have helped him in many ways.

But I want to talk to you for a few minutes about the future rather than the past. The solution of the problems of personnel management, in government or out, will never be solved and the answers found and applied in the sense that they can be folded up and laid away on the shelf, for we are dealing with people who are affected by every variable wind that blows across our landscape; the field of our interests, and the trend of thought and action even today is against our program rather than for it. If we are to make progress, as we must, in our forward progress, there is, there will always be, hard work ahead. Prepare for that, make no little plans, for little plans do not stir the imagination of people nor gather friends or support. Think big, think straight and don't be turned aside by the opposition of any individual or group. Give your new secretary, whoever he may be, your support and encouragement and help him put this large membership you have to work on the many facets of your problems.

When we began we had problems spelled in capital letters, both officialdom and people generally. We had little help in numbers and few people cared. You have scores of professionals in addition to the large group of people now working in the personnel field in your membership — a mass of talent waiting to be used. Don't let that talent get away from you. Remember that if you neglect it or do not use it, it will lose its interest and drift away.

You are the heirs of the past, of all of those who thought and worked and struggled in that past to find the place of the personnel in administration. There is an old and honored adage of the long past, namely "The young men will see visions and the old men will dream dreams." I am not dreaming today. I am trying to tell you once again something of the problems we found along the way in the hope that this reminder will be helpful to you and others as I leave the active field.

I have read and reread the report of your annual committee and the letter of your retiring president transmitted to this association. These are significant documents, and they contain the landmarks and the guidelines of further advancement. The authors of these documents have seen the vision we saw; they are saying that they will follow in our footsteps. I warn you though to keep in mind that the problems you face are greater than ours were in size and complexity. You will find the going slow and difficult but do not be turned aside.

Unfortunately we are a divided people today, no matter how many excuses and alibis we find coming from high places. We are in one of the danger periods of our nation, but we will survive. There are other, many parts of the personnel administration that I must pass over. I mention only the important ones. Existing positions must be classified as to their requirements, their duties and their responsibilities. The question of establishing new positions and eliminating old positions no longer needed must be given attention. Compensation schedules for every position in the service in keeping with the going rate of pay in business and commercial enterprise, the degree of the responsibility and duties carried, the possibilities of advancement and the social worth of the service must be determined. Adequate machinery is necessary for recruiting properly qualified persons who possess the industry, the integrity and the ability to render capable and acceptable service. Uniform and just procedure must be established for the regulation of employees in the service, designed to maintain their morale and their interest.

We cannot find these answers by argument, by reciting our differences. We can do it only by togetherness and determination. We can go back to ancient notions of fighting crime by an eye for an eye, a tooth for a tooth, a life for a life, all larded in part by sound judgment and mercy. We can get on our way toward the solution of inflation by and through agreement and action. We need most a new birth of freedom — an earnest effort by all of us to get back to the fundamentals already worked out and tested, and thus we can prevail. Deny the offerings of smooth talking false prophets; we have them yet — our Neros.

CHAPTER 9

The New Jersey Proving Ground

Druz: New Jersey has had a remarkable history in its success with its personnel management problems. This success has been accomplished here by the hard work and the leadership of Dr. Charles P. Messick.

We have not held to the level he set for the state and all America. We are trying to bring back the accomplishments of those early years; so I have invited Dr. Messick to come back to us, tell the story as only he can tell it, in order that we can add it to our museum and thus have the story from the man whose genius and foresight marked our state as the unchallenged leader in this field, in this conversation between the Director who made history here and me, William Druz, the present Director of the Department.

I am proud of the fact that Dr. Messick appointed me to his staff. I shall always be grateful to him for the opportunity that put me in the way of following in his footsteps.

AUTHOR'S NOTE: The following is the transcript of a tape-recorded conversation, as an oral history project, between myself and William Druz, then Director of the State of New Jersey Department of Personnel Management. The interview took place on May 10, 1972. All questions, indicated by a "Q", are those of Druz; and all answers, indicated by an "A", are my responses.

Q. Dr. Messick, I have learned that you are often called "Mr. Civil Service" here in our state and, as a matter of fact, all over America. How did you acquire that imposing title?

A. I didn't acquire it; like Topsy, I guess, "it just growed up."

I do not claim that I deserve such a friendly title, but I must admit that by reason of my work here in New Jersey I got some attention at home, and as the seeming success that we were having here spread to other agencies and widened to the whole country, it came about as a compliment on our work.

Q. Dr. Messick, the first New Jersey Civil Service law was enacted, as you say, in 1908 to become effective in October of that year. What brought it about in these early days?

A. There had been brewing for some years a growing opposition to "boss leadership." The movement against that leadership and attending waste was centered in Essex County and the surrounding area. The movement was mainly in the Republican Party, for New Jersey was then a Republican state and the local group, which was pressing for the change, was known as "The New Idea Party." I shall try to avoid naming names because it would not be fair to name two or three people involved when there were many. In this instance, however, I think I must name the two leaders. They were Senator Everett Colby, the then state senator from Essex County, and his friend and colleague, Senator Austin Colgate from Hudson County.

Bossism, you know, is an old affliction. It still is evident. It was dominant here then, even destructive, and it yet goes on and on.

Q. When and how did you enter the picture?

A. I came into the service by accident. The chief examiner and secretary of the Civil Service Commission was looking for a part-time assistant examiner. He happened to get hold of my name. He asked me to come to see him and he asked me to undertake the job.

Q. How did you start?

A. Well I was obliged to start from the bottom. I looked over the tests that had been given, and gathered data and information from New York City, New York State, and other places. I went to see Mr. George Wales, then Chief Examiner of the U. S. Civil Service Commission, whose wife happened to be a native of New Jersey, and started in. All my life I have been used to work, hard work. I just worked. In a short time I took over the whole examining activity, besides doing graduate work at the University of Pennsylvania, teaching, coaching, and building up the Trenton evening schools as director. I worked seven days and seven nights a week. I kept this up all my working life. I have not yet learned how to be idle.

Q. What was the attitude of the appointing authorities to these new limitations on their appointive power?

A. About the same as it is today, a little more violent. They seemed to think then, as a great many think now, that the merit system is all right for the other departments but not for themselves. And this attitude lingers on as you may have noticed.

Q. How do you compare the calibre of the average public employee in those early years with the average employee today?

A. That is a hard question. There were many employees in every department and dedicated employees who worked hard, felt a personal interest in their department or agency, and did their best. In my time, particularly in the 20's and 30's, most employers, officers, supervisors, and employees offered, I think, a greater devotion to their work, appreciated their protection and opportunity, and were better qualified.

There are several answers as to why this was so. It must be remembered that as a people we had been greatly chastened in 1917-1918; and when we were beginning to forget and things were moving back toward normal we began again to make headway. By the time the dark days of '29 and the early '30's came along, we had gained a good measure of confidence and respect from officers, politicians, departmental authorities, and the public. We fought off the many proposals made to suspend the merit system entirely and we were able to maintain the system. We had made great progress in the extension of the civil service system. These were the great days of progress in the service not only in New Jersey but throughout the country.

I suppose I should add that I had become the leader of the Civil Service Association, and the merit system supporters looked to me as the leader of the movement through its Civil Service Assembly during those years, later known as the Public Personnel Association, and now the International Personnel Management Association.

Q. Now that you have said that, what brought this about?

A. A number of things. I suppose the main reasons were hard work, fair dealing, and staying a little ahead of the crowds. We had built up a great deal of goodwill. We had built also a small but strong staff, that was willing to work as I worked. We furnished governors, one after another, with intelligent, detailed data each year as budget making time approached, from which they would know what needed to be done, what departmental authorities wanted and what we thought they really needed. From these data they could and did determine their whole personnel and management policies for the state.

We had also built up a cordial relationship with both houses of the legislature. It was the practice then, as you know, for both the Senate and the Assembly to make appointments, allotted to them to carry on the work of the legislature, of friends and political workers without much regard as to qualifications for the job. A clerk may have been a good friend but knew nothing about the duties he was expected to perform; as a matter of fact, he may not show up except on payday. To meet this situation we began to send qualified clerks and stenographers to help out, to do the clerical work really of both houses of the legislature. This became a regular practice amounting to a demand. It continues to this day. It is economical, develops goodwill and should be continued. As far as I know that practice still prevails.

Then again, every senator and every assemblyman, especially the new ones, always had a disgruntled constituent who failed in an examination, did not get appointed, wanted a promotion, and who was generally unhappy. I made it a point to see all of those who came to our office. I showed him or her the records. I explained why we were obliged to say "no" and showed our side of the story. I told him why we were obliged to take the action we did in each particular case. I would continue to do the same thing if I were in harness today.

Q. What other services did you render to governors, senators, assemblymen, and committee members that you have not already mentioned?

A. I would hesitate to answer this question if I had not been away from here so long, but few if any remember.

I did a great deal of writing for several governors. I acted as consultant to many legislative committees and wrote their reports. For example, I wrote the relief plan for the city of Trenton, the first, so far as I know, in the state, then extended it to the county. Finally, I wrote the statewide relief act and had it ready for introduction when Governor Larson was obliged to create a statewide plan. He named Chester Barnard, then president of the New Jersey State Telephone Company, as State Director. During my time I wrote more state papers than any person, certainly by or before that time, and I suspect since those early years. I rewrote the Civil Service Rules and a proposed Civil Service Statute in '29 and '30. If you will read a copy of that bill as first introduced, you will find your own authority outlined there.

Q. How did you get along with your civil service commissioners in all this work?

A. Well, let me answer it this way. I served longer in this office than any other person living or dead, in any personnel agency, in any state or local governmental unit in the country and retired voluntarily and on my own action on July 6, 1949. I should add, in fairness, that this was not because everybody was happy. At times, a new commissioner would come in with the notion that my actions needed looking into. I bided my time. I always followed the plan of reporting to the commissioners as individuals and in meetings and explained everything that had been done as clearly as possible and the reasons therefor, and then let them make up their own minds. So far as I know, no commissioner ever left the Commission who was not my friend and supporter.

Q. The recent report of the Governor's Study Commission makes some rather harsh statements about the Civil Service Commission. A new body has been created to overrule, it would seem, the Commission. I think that this inquiry would not be complete without your comments.

A. This whole matter is controversial. I am against the proposal that the testing of applicants for the public service should be taken out of the hands of the Director of the Civil Service Commission as now constituted and left to the appointing authority. I am against any other agency that stands between the Civil Service Department and the appointing authorities or the appointees. That agency should be abolished. In these times when few people apply for examinations and when there is no competition, the principle falls. But those of us who have lived long enough know that such a situation here involved will not last, and that the public service employment with the pay levels and increasing fringe benefits attached will again be much sought after, that true competitive testing will return, and that the real advantages of a proper handling of personnel matters will accrue to the state as well as to the general public. There is no doubt but the merit system properly manned and properly applied will insure better public administration and will save money besides.

It may be well to remember that old notion "to the victor belongs the spoils" is yet lurking in the minds of some of the appointing authorities, of wanting to make their own selection of their own employees as they did before the civil service system was instituted. It is safe to say, however, that that time is past and that it will not come back.

With respect to the elimination of the commission itself, while the numerous commissioners for whom I served supported my efforts to a high degree, they lent little help to those technical matters that were then necessary to fix in the minds of governors, members of the legislature, and appointing authorities and supervisory personnel, the acceptance of our personnel practice. Civil service commissions were originally set up to control and in large measure to stop political and personal appointment and arbitrary dismissal of capable and devoted employees. The federal commission was set up on the basis of not quite trusting the President, apparently, to appoint a high ranking director to plan, develop and maintain a constructive system. Yet the President appointed three men who might be politically motivated and frequently were defeated candidates of the party for whom consolation prizes must be found. The states and municipalities that adopted the merit system statutes followed the form of the federal government and no one can truthfully say that that system is entirely eliminated. It has been crippled and reduced, but vigilance here is the price of safety. You will find traces of it, pretty plain traces if you should look into the records, and note the reasons for the appointments to positions in the unclassified service, that is, those offices and the few positions where appointments are made at the will of the appointing officers. In one of your cities the mayor has appointed a milkman to a department that deals with engineering problems while proclaiming his support of the merit system.

In the old days when the merit system was always being attacked, on trial, and threatened to be weakened in one way or another, it had to be defended. I do not say that these attacks were personal or there might have been some failure in the work and decisions of the personnel department. I am saying now that the position of merit system administrator requires a capable, well-trained individual who should stand nearer to the Governor than any other directing officer in his administration. I have said this many times during my service and not without risk of being misunderstood. The system is now established, its responsibilities and limitations are known, and it is just about as reasonable to appoint three or five Secretaries of State, or

State Treasurers or multiple department heads to any department, rather than one director to any major department of government.

Q. What about hearings by employees who feel they have been unjustly treated, punished, or dismissed by a department head?

A. The record of your present commission and every commission from the time, at least, when the number of employees and the service grew to large proportions, shows a lag in the holding of hearings and asking decisions. It has been reported in recent weeks that you are now two years behind in keeping this activity current and that after all the efforts that you have in recent months made you are yet as far behind as ever.

Q. The hearing of grievances of both employees and departmental officials seeking to make changes for any good cause, who should do it?

A. The Civil Service Commission is not nor should it be a court. Yet our commission and most other similar commissions in the nation have assumed that they are courts. They cannot seem to get away from the idea. When a hearing is asked, the department should promptly determine whether, from the facts and circumstances in hand, it is warranted. If so, it should be investigated quickly and fairly, and a decision made without delay. A long, drawn out hearing is not needed; what is required are facts. One individual can do that through qualified investigators or examiners. In our country, anybody can sue anybody, anytime for anything, and it would seem now everybody is doing just that.

The old adage, "Justice delayed is justice denied," is one of the eternal verities in our restless world. These delays are disturbing and upsetting to the victim; bad for the individual or department involved; and many times it involves also an unwarranted expense to a department and the government itself. Under our present system, some cases sometimes run on for years, because of the act of an improper employee or by an act of an impetuous departmental authority. This is not the way to use public money or maintain effective administration. Any ordinary appeal, so far as the personnel department is concerned, can and should be settled in thirty days. I repeat, the personnel department is not a court. If there must be a court trial, the aggrieved party should go to the courts in the first place.

Q. What are your thoughts on the employee association?

A. I believe in the organization of public employees. I was a member of the first group of state employees that met secretly in a downtown office in Trenton. I knew and worked with Ben Selingmen of Newark, Dick Donovan, Jack Finn, and Frank Walker of Jersey City, and Charlie Clayton of Trenton. These men worked openly and unselfishly for the observance of the civil service laws and the proper protection of public employees. I have known John Goff and Harry Walsh from the beginning. Following the changing times, John has gone further than I believe is necessary or wise, but then I cling perhaps to the old ways. But John and Harry have been stand-up fighters for what they considered proper employee problems.

I yet carry a membership card in the State Employees Association.

Q. Do you believe that public employees should strike or have the right to strike?

A. No. I do not consider that government's handling of public employees' interests and appeals have always been right or equitable, but I believe that, by and large, our public employees are given more consideration than those of any other country or government, or employees in private enterprise. I believe, too, that with all its faults and failures our form of government is the best for this nation and for all Americans. I do not believe that any employee should refuse to perform the duties assigned to him and for which he was employed. I knew most of the early leaders who advocated the right to strike, and I have seen the struggle all along for recognition of this so-called right.

To me, it is elemental that only governing legislative bodies can bargain away monies for which appropriations have not already been made. I have said throughout the years, many times in many places, that if I had a grievance that could not be adjusted to my satisfaction, I would resign. I would not strike against my government.

Q. Employees in private enterprise have the right to strike and in many states and local jurisdictions and in some parts of the federal service employees are granted the privilege and have exercised it. Would you deny to a public employee what he may have as a private citizen?

A. Yes.

Q. Why?

A. No person is compelled to work for his government. He seeks that service and on seeking it he accepts totally or formally the limitations that his government places upon every public employee whatever his rank or station. If he finds at any time that he is not being treated according to his rights or to his worth, and he finds no way to bridge the gap, then he is free to resign and should do so. I have thought a great deal about this problem. I ask no one to accept my own conclusions in this matter. If you will go to your history books, you will find that any government that cannot or will not enforce its own laws and rules and regulations does not endure. I want to make our government better. I do not want to destroy it.

Q. There has been in recent years a great deal of talk about second class citizens. Do you think that public employees are second class citizens without this right?

A. No. As you know, I have spent most of my working life in the public service. I never accepted any such classification. I felt myself to be a privileged citizen. I was working in a position that offered an opportunity to serve every citizen in the improvement of the operation and functioning of my government and his, and incidentally to aid in the encouragement to other governmental jurisdictions to follow our example. I had opportunities to go into other fields as you have. I did not accept them so I could stay with what I considered my "unfinished job."

Q. Let me refer back to a matter that we touched upon in the earlier part of this discussion. The point I want you to discuss is the failure of yourself or the commission to get the legislature to include by statute a provision that every public jurisdiction, special state department, district, municipality, county, or township in the state come into the merit system.

A. I held, and I believe the Civil Service Commission believed at all times, that we had a greater load than we could carry at any given time within our appropriations, and that these outside jurisdictions were coming into the merit system even faster than we could handle them. We had and yet have, I believe, 690 separate jurisdictions in the state. More than half of these were so small that they had so few employees and the pay was so small there was little advantage to anybody to bring them into the service. Most of their job problems were settled over the backyard fence where the women voters talk out their problems, and on the street corners where male voters gather in the evening to settle public questions. Generally, we thought that we would serve best by devoting all of our efforts in trying to do a better job on what we had.

Q. Back about 1909 and 1910 the legislature enacted a law requiring that election officers at every polling place in the state must take a civil service test to qualify for the post, but the requirement was soon repealed. Why?

A. This was another of these reform ideas that comes up from time to time. There developed scattered complaints about the quality and qualifications of election officers appointed to assist voters on election, to hold and assure safekeeping of ballot boxes, to count votes, and to make correct and authentic returns to the proper county officers. These people were selected and named by local county officials of the two ruling parties. There were opportunities for wheeling and dealing of course, and there were abuses. The press gave the matter publicity and the enactment of the law followed. As I recall, the Governor appointed a new officer in each county to supervise the work and a general supervisor for the state, and the general supervisor had no understanding of what to do and how to do it, and no capacity to restrict anyone. Some added money was assigned to the Civil Service Department, and the supervisor had a desk near mine.

At that time I was not yet on a full-time basis, but the job of preparing tests was assigned to me, in addition to the other work I was carrying. I think that the tests were fairly good. The payroll was so small that there was scarcely any competition, and many applicants were not qualified. The net results were that in many polling places there were no applicants and in others not enough who qualified to fill the number of jobs available. The plan was a failure and that provision of the law was repealed. Election machinery of the state can be set up and the department can be manned so that there may be provided qualified people filling these positions. The pay would have to be increased; the qualified personnel would have to be brought in through countywide competition and assigned wherever needed. There qualifying tests could be held and qualified personnel provided. At that time we had not gotten far enough along to cancel out political influence in elections, and I see little desire to do it now.

Q. I note throughout the records, annual reports, and announcements that in the name of the commission references are made to a "zoning system," which continues more or less to this day. What does this mean, why was it established, and do you consider it useful?

A. There is no provision in the statutes for a zoning system. At the beginning there were three, later four, and now five commissioners. Soon after the establishment of the Civil Service Commission, Newark, Essex County, Jersey City, and a little later Hudson County adopted the provisions of the statute, and a great many administrative matters needed almost daily attention. As a matter of convenience to the departmental authorities, to employees, to prospective applicants, and to the public, the commission set up a branch office in the Newark City Hall. A secretary was named and matters relating to the general area were handled by the Chief Examiner under the general oversight of the commissioner residing in the area. As the public service multiplied, offices were set up in Elizabeth for routine service, Paterson, and Camden with the remaining commissioners assigned to the state at Trenton. At one time, Dr. John Dynely Prince, an outstanding scholar, a professor at Columbia University, and a former State Senator from Passaic County, and residing in the area near the New York State border, was named President of the Commission and, on his own preference, he was the Zone Commissioner at Paterson.

As time passed, the commissioners were assigned to an office in these several zones where they resided, or one convenient to them. These assigned commissioners soon began to feel that matters arising in their particular areas should be handled or at least presented to them. They felt they could make a decision either binding, conditional, or agree to take the matters up at the next meeting. When some official or employee in the zone area came to a commissioner in another zone, the commissioner would as a matter of course refer him to the zone commissioner assigned to his area. The results as a whole were unsatisfactory and caused more trouble than good. Anyway, under the present statutes, the responsibilities now belong to the President and Chief Examiner and serve little other purpose than a place where a commissioner may go and have a desk and a chair.

Q. There are many other matters we could discuss with profit and other questions on which I should like to have your views. An important part of an effective personnel program — examinations, their content and character, eligible lists, certifications, appointments, service rating, training, and the like — are areas I'd like to touch upon. A series of general questions on public or legislative attacks, a new law, the effects of war and peace, unfinished business and the future are additional areas we should discuss. I shall jump around somewhat as new questions

come to my mind or I find that I want to pursue a question already asked. I shall try, however, to follow a somewhat orderly procedure. In 1919, you say in the annual report that some opposition and attacks have developed and some of them have been partly successful. What was in your mind?

A. Without access to the report you speak of I would remind you that we had just passed through the great and destructive World War I. In that year, 1919, we were trying to get back from a war basis to a peace basis, which meant sudden and drastic changes throughout our government and our whole economic system. During the war period, it was urged that every normal peace-time activity should be stopped, that departmental heads should be permitted to appoint staff as they decided necessary, and pay what they wished. We were able to accept some of these proposals. We gave a little to get a lot. When a new movement occurred either from within the government or without, we would call a conference to discuss the matters to gain time. We succeeded in forestalling these demands for the time being. The responsibilities of all of this fell on me, and many times I felt pretty much alone. Although some of the commissioners were half convinced that we should surrender, they did agree that I should stick to my guns; and with the help I could muster from the employee associations and more conservative departmental heads, we were able to keep the merit system intact.

During this period, raises in pay had been delayed, and both employees and departmental authorities were anxious for immediate relief. As a department we checked appropriations' balances for two or three years back and found that many of the departments, as the budget neared its end, played the old game of transferring funds from one account to another where they could be spent, lest the up-coming appropriation committee discovered them and became stubborn about more money for the next year. This is an old game, as you know, and it is yet popular and working. With the data in hand, I submitted my plan first to my commission, then to the Governor, showing that by pooling all departmental balances — and with very little, if any, additional funds — we could give a bonus payment to all state employees. With approval of the Governor, I prepared detailed and exact regulations, setting forth the condition and the amounts that should be allotted to every class and individual, which the Governor approved and directed me to carry out. I held a departmental conference; the unbelievers were not convinced but they approved the plan; then it went to the legislature which adopted it. As you may expect, it was harder to distribute than to get, and the doubters were hardest to satisfy.

Close on the heels of this, the returning veterans asked for jobs in the public service without examination or reference to their qualifications. There was both sentiment and need attached to this request, and had this plan been accepted, it would have set back the merit system and the Civil Service Commission's work indefinitely, and our building of it to that date would have been destroyed. We worked out a compromise. The chairman issued a ringing statement, proposing a plan (I never wrote a better one). The proposed plan warded off absolute response to the claims for veterans, giving certain credit points for overseas veterans, and placing those who passed the regular tests at the top of the list. It did help the veterans and again saved the system. To the extent that the best qualified were likely to be appointed, it was of course in the best interest of the service as a whole. But we did owe a great deal to these men who stood in the trenches, ruined their health, and were able to come back and pick up the threads of their civil life. Now the veterans of our Asian wars are coming back. I suspect that any radical changes here may be long delayed and will again be renewed in other jurisdictions throughout the country.

Q. What was meant by reference to the under-use of the promotion principle?

A. This is a healthy protest; promotion from one class to another is always in order, and when there are not more than three, and it is known that these employees are qualified, promotion may be made without examination. The protests usually come from those in lower classes. Of course, we should see to it that "the best shall serve the state." I am not convinced that we will do better by acceding to these requests at least now.

Q. In going over some of the earlier annual reports, there were statements that implied that something happened to cause new classification plans to be prepared.

A. Nothing in particular had happened under the rules, and we were expected to go over our rules for the state service, to prepare classification plans for local governments. In local governments, pay scales and pay increases were determined by the local authorities. We did have authority to see that there was equity in the plans. In a considerable number of cases, this authority was abused and the normal rights of departmental employees were ignored. That authority should be given to the commission, but working with the commission on local government. The 1930 law, as I first wrote it, provided the same authority over local governments as in the state. That section was not approved.

Q. What happened in 1929 when the old commission was removed from office and a new commission was appointed?

A. This was the result of a growing problem in Hudson County where it was reported that the payrolls of some employees were not being certified by our department before payment. There was a legislative committee appointed and we were directed to make an investigation and furnish the data as far as they could be shown to that committee. We did so. The commission did not do well in handling themselves either individually or collectively. They were removed by the Governor. I would say, in passing, the offenses were of no great consequence, but were illegal. The main group of these employees were at the City's reservoir, which was twenty-five or thirty miles away, and water must be piped down to the City. A few of the twenty or so employees were sent up from Jersey City, but there was not adequate housing and most of the employees were recruited from nearby areas. The new commission was now anxious to get off to a good start and justify the changes. I was obliged naturally to acquaint them with the duties of their office. I did so in this case as I tried to do in my whole experience. I reported every important act in the succeeding meeting, explained what I thought was the right and legal thing to do, and the legislation needed if any, and the probable difficulty involved. Their batting average was high. You are asking why the change in the length and format of the annual report just following this change in the commission. The statute provides for an annual report. I put the report together and while the new commission could not say it was its report, they signed the report as the law required.

Q. There seems to be a matter of a new law, what about this?

A. As Chief Examiner, I was busy as always. The then laws were a mass of amendments and additions to the original statute. I had long intended to write a new law, and I did so. I wrote it in as plain words as I could and left out all "provided, however"s. I had it introduced, and with slight changes except for the matter of pay in local governments, the revision was adopted. In the recodification in later years, the professional codifiers did violence to my unlawyer-like language, but I got in the authority intended with the amendments necessary to get the bill passed, and with a little appeasement to the new commission, we got this important landmark. I was able to add to my staff. With regard to Dr. Haupt's appointment — she was working at the time for what was then called the Bureau of Public Personnel Administration, one of my step-children, of which I was the unpaid chairman. It is now called the Public Personnel Association as you know. She was a capable lady. I needed some help that did not require a period of training. I merely transferred her from the Bureau to work with me for a few months.

Q. What basically was different in the new law as compared with the old law?

A. The old law was a compilation of provisions of the federal law, the New York State law, the Commonwealth of Massachusetts law, the New York City law and some original provisions designed to fit New Jersey's own situation. It was written by Theodore H. Backus, Assistant Attorney General. He was an able lawyer and did a good job for that time. It had been amended and changed so many times that it was almost impossible to get two attorneys to agree as to its proper meaning. I wanted a statute that would be clear and definite in its meaning.

A number of people and organizations have written so-called model laws, but most of these people or representatives of organizations have never stood on the firing line, trying to run a large and complicated merit system, and stand there long enough to be challenged on the results.

Q. That is interesting. I want to get back to this matter of tests and their development. When you entered the picture there was little published material on tests. What should be their content and how could the tests prove much of anything? How did you go about this business of writing questions?

A. Well, I had gotten used to tests in school and college, and as a teacher I had had some experience in writing and scoring them. The watchword of the civil service reformers, you may know, was "keep the rascals out." They proposed to do that by written tests, even though the usual test had little if any relation to the contemplated duties to be performed. I began to see, as did some other examiners in the field, that a test should be on the duties and responsibilities of the job and the qualifications a competitor should have. I included an oral interview as part of all tests, where the duties of an appointee from the resulting roster involved contact with the public. So our tests were made up generally of these factors or parts: (1) education, training and experience; (2) duties; (3) physical and medical standards, where these were factors; and (4) oral interview. We took extra care in assigning weights to each of these factors or parts.

Our efforts, perhaps, were weak and results were uncertain, but we kept trying; we learned by doing, and we began to attract some attention in the field. Our fixed rule, which was never changed during my administration, was "try to make the next test better than the one before."

Q. I believe there was no classification of jobs when you began? Who named the job to be filled and the qualifications therefor?

A. The appointing authority. He was naturally anxious to limit competition and he might say: "I must have a stenographer with six months training in educational work," and we would have to include that in our requirements or get into an argument. We kept struggling against unreasonably limiting requirements and finally succeeded. For a long time now the personnel agency has set the requirements, except in some physical requirements such as height and weight, and minimum and maximum entering age, height and weight of police officers, uniformed firemen, guards, rangers and comparable classes. There were always attacks on oral ratings, of course, claims of prejudice, favoritism, etc., and this could happen and did, of course. My answer always was: That could be, but the people who hire workmen of all kinds including professionals everywhere for all kinds of positions do it, and we will continue to follow this course, that I shall not undertake to change this practice, and furthermore I am going to continue the practice until I am prevented from doing so.

Q. There was, in the late nineties, a great deal of discussion of economy and efficiency in business and industry, and professional efficiency engineers began to emerge?

A. This was true, but these claims were of little use. Some of these people were neither efficient nor engineers, but they were on the right track, and today, as you know, they have standing and do render good service. Then we had the sociologists who were going to fit all the round pegs into the round holes and all the square pegs in the square holes. They, too, made advances in the discovery and adjustments of the human animal. Then came the man and wife team who found the one best way to do things. The cheaper by the dozen family group, Mrs. Elfrith still lives at the time of this recording. She was the able one of the family, and then there came Robert Hutchins, the boy president of the University of Chicago. I knew him rather well at that time. He had some very good ideas for the improvement of the University, and particularly the faculty. He did more for his staff than most of them had ever hoped for, and some of those who merited the advancement he got for them disliked him so much he finally resigned. He was and is a brilliant man, but I think he has gotten beyond his depth. He yet lives, and now heads a self-perpetuating group who are deliberating the destinies of mankind.

Then, too, we have the economists and psychologists. The economists tend to stand apart and look. I think they should have had a much greater influence on government than they have had. They do not seem anxious to get down into the trenches and on the firing line and stay there until the job is done. Our experience with them in Washington has not been altogether successful. It seems to me that as a learned group they have not contributed as much to the improvement and functioning of government as they should have done. The psychologists have made a real contribution to those of us in the testing field. They reminded us again that big things are made up of a lot of little things and that if we want to understand them we turn them back to little things so that we can better understand them. They gave us the short answer tests — used everywhere for intelligence measurement and for many purposes.

Q. What was your experience with the short answer tests in the civil service field?

A. We used them, those that are ready-made for parts of our tests, and designed some for some job groups. They, however, are difficult to prepare and time consuming and when we did prepare them ourselves we had no means of testing them out. We did try to measure the results of our tests. For example: the results of any test as to scores or ratings obtained is supposed to rise like a pyramid with a broad base and rising in a somewhat straight diminishing line to a rounded top and descend on the other side in the reverse of the ascending line. One of my staff men studied the results of our police and prison officer tests over the years and drew diagrams showing these results as the basis for his doctoral dissertation. As he proceeded he brought to me the graphs and parts of his writings on his work. My question was often, "Your research is interesting and I would like to believe that your graphs are significant but what do they really show? Where should you pitch your cutoff point between eligibles and failures?" He could not answer these questions and I have not seen answers that I would accept yet. I encouraged him to keep at it, and in due course the final oral examination for his doctorate was accepted by one of our good and large universities. I was invited to sit with the university board for the candidates for their degrees. I hope you will permit me to add that my staff member did well as compared to the group in other disciplines, and his dissertation was accepted. May I add further that our boy retired, after a long and useful career in public personnel work and as a university professor.

Q. That is interesting, did you lose other staff members to other agencies?

A. Oh yes. For years my office was a sort of training school for administrators and technicians for other personnel agencies. I sent one to Michigan who later ended his career at Hartford, Connecticut; two or three to New York State, one of whom just retired as Director of Personnel at New Orleans and who continues as a university professor; one to the Tennessee Valley Authority; one to New York Mutual Life Insurance Company who became Vice President of Personnel and Public Relations; and several others of whom I lost contact went to other agencies. One is yet at work as a Senior Fellow at Brookings Institution. I think we may say that New Jersey did fairly well in influencing personnel practice and our way of doing things throughout the nation.

Q. The classification of jobs and the addition of qualification requirements, a statement of the duties to be performed, and the pay rates marked a decided advance in the whole selective procedure. You were a part of this earlier development. How did it begin and who were involved?

A. The one man in this country most involved was E. O. Griffenhagen of Chicago. He is yet alive. As a young man, he was an employee of the Chicago Civil Service Commission, at a time when Chicago was having a government trying to do something for the city. He was assigned to straighten out the personnel system for the park system. In his work, he came to the point of naming the jobs of the employees and proposing pay rates. He noted that there were some positions that were the same and some different from all the others. His problem was putting those alike together. He hit upon the word "class," not by the name of the employee, but of the work they were doing. We now say that that is simple; anyone would know that. It was an important discovery, nevertheless. The Chinese had something like that arrangement some thousand of years ago and New Zealand had it also, but we did not know that. This classification and grouping of positions was notable in the public service in America and became the foundation of all you are doing here and all we are doing everywhere. The time as I recall was 1911. I was struggling with tests then. At a meeting in New York City of the Commissioners of Civil Service in 1913, Mr. Griffenhagen was given a place on the program to explain this new way. I was at that meeting. We got acquainted and became friends, and that friendship has lasted to this day. Soon thereafter he joined the Arthur Young Company, an outstanding accountant firm, which is still in existence. Two or three years later he established his own company — Griffenhagen & Associates, which specialized in making classification, organizational, pay, personnel studies of all kinds, and the installation of proposed plans. One of his early assistants, J. L. Jacobs, set up a company in his own name, and he too has been successful; he still lives and his company is yet active. Jacobs did our classification study in 1916. I worked with him and installed the classification here in New Jersey.

Now we find individuals and firms everywhere offering expertise in any line and for any purpose one can think of, and the odd part of it all now is that almost every government, big and little, hires one or more of these people or firms to do special studies about something whenever they want to take almost any action on what the governing bodies consider of some importance. At the moment, New Jersey has the fever. In my time we did these jobs ourselves and better because we knew our territory and our people. I worked from time to time with Griffenhagen and, as you know, I had my own company after my retirement here in 1949.

In 1919-22, Griffenhagen contracted with the Canadian government to make a comprehensive study of the government organization and personnel of Canada, the first and largest undertaking of its kind ever attempted and, incidentally, the most successful one. He proposed wide reorganizational changes, most of which were accepted and implemented. I extended my vacation in '19 or '20 and worked on that project for a time. I met there Fred Telford, a member of the Griffenhagen Staff, an able man, restless and full of ideas. He became the center man of the staff and added the description of duties and proposed qualification requirements, and so completed the job specifications that we have used since then and yet use with some refinements and minor changes.

After that Canadian experience, Telford worked for me and under my supervision as one of my associates. His contribution to the advancement of personnel administration has been equal to that of any other person in the field. He died, as you may know, four or five years ago.

Q. Nowadays we read about and hear about training in and for the public service. Did you have what might be called such training?

A. We had a sort of vestibule training in our department, when we added a new staff member. I would have a meeting of the staff members with whom he or she would work. I assigned such new members to an experienced member of the group as a sort of caretaker-instructor to work with the added member and instruct him or her until he or she got acquainted with the fellow workers and became oriented as we would say today.

I favor training before and after entrance into the service, but I believe more in performance. One learns by doing more than by listening.

I do not want to be misunderstood. I got my training the hard way. But you can't make leaders merely by training a mediocre individual. You can train him to do what he can do, but the true leader does not come up that way. He must have the element of leadership in himself. I believe you call it "id" nowadays.

Q. As I examine the records available to me, it appears that progress was intermittent in New Jersey and, of course, that is the history both in government and in other activities. Did this happen in New Jersey?

A. Yes.

Q. When, then, did that take place there?

A. We had our greatest advances in the 1920 to 1930 decade. When we settled down to a peacetime situation after 1918 and turned our thinking and actions to peacetime pursuits, business and industry were anxious to get back to normal business activity and profit. Government, too, was just as anxious and ready to get back on a peacetime basis. You can't remember, perhaps, but you may have read that that was a war to end war. We had saved the framework of the merit system as I have said above. We needed to put flesh back on the bones. We had debts such as government had never known here. We seemed to be almost a new people, but we were not heroic. It was necessity rather than virtue that compelled our attitude and our action.

Q. How did we get into this action so far as the public service was concerned?

A. I rarely talk about it, but it is a part of the civil service story. In 1919 or 1920, we had gotten to a place in our own progress where the civil service people began to want to hear more about our work here, of what we were doing and how we were doing it. At a meeting of the Assembly of Civil Service Commissioners in Rochester in 1919, I was given a place on the program to tell something of our work.

The night before the formal meetings opened, fifteen or twenty of the older leaders — nearly all commissioners — met for an informal discussion on their problems. One of the number who had had a longer and wider experience than the others chaired the meeting. He opened the meeting, outlined the reasons for it and spoke about some of his own problems back in New York. Then one after another of the commissioners spoke in the same strain. It was the same story. They were having trouble, they might lose their jobs, and things were bad generally. The longer they talked the more uncomfortable I got, and when the chairman broke in finally to say, "Yes, we are not doing too well, not as well as we know how to do, but if we should do that, we would lose our jobs." I got up and blurted out with more disappointment than diplomacy saying, "I have not had the experience that you men have had, but have been at it long enough to become convinced that the things we are trying to do are of vital importance to our governments. I think it is more important than you or me. You say that you do not do as well as you know what to do; if that is the way you feel, I think it might not be too bad if you did lose your jobs." That about ended the meeting, and to my surprise and relief nearly all of them gathered around me and all began to say, it seemed, "You are right." They had a new leader. Their question was: "What shall we do?" I said, "I don't know much about it but there are foundations, the Rockefeller Foundation for example, that offer funds for research and study. Appoint a committee to go into the matter and see what we can do."

The next day I sat with a few of the group and wrote the resolution to be presented at a later meeting. I left before that meeting, but the resolution was adopted. A committee was appointed and I was designated as chairman and we were in business. Two years later I was able to report to the annual meeting that we had been granted a study fund that would be continued for some years if our Assembly approved our efforts. I was elected chairman of the Assembly in 1922.

The Bureau of Public Personnel was set up under the aegis of the Institute of Government in Washington. I was named to represent the civil service field. Fred Telford was made secretary of the organization and we went to work.

The Bureau continued for ten years. Telford traveled over the country carrying encouragement and technical aid to personnel agencies everywhere. I stayed in New Jersey working out what I considered the place and the part of the personnel agency in government. By the middle of the decade I thought I had something to say and that it was time to talk about it. At the 1926 Assembly meeting, I said among other advancing practices that it is time to recognize the fact that the personnel agency, if it is to do its job, must be an integral part of the government, that this practice of the personnel agency of handing its rulings and actions over the barrier or under it, or around it, always on the outside of things, must be ended, and that it must accept and be accepted as an integral part of the administrative process. This had come at last to us in New Jersey. Going further, I said that government required and must have enough qualified employees to do the work of government that needed to be done, properly organized, properly supervised, adequately but not extravagantly paid, and fairly treated and doing a fair day's work everyday; and therefore there should be only as many such workers as were needed to do the work that needed to be done. You must know that one of the substantial wastes in government is keeping agencies whose duties have been assumed by other agencies and who continue to do things because they have been done before. Of course, these situations continue in many places and will continue maybe for all time, but the idea is recognized. These proposals were accepted. They have become a part of the philosophy and the ideals of our Assembly and accepted in some measure in many jurisdictions.

Q. What further moves, if any, should be a part of this recital?

A. One of the things that I noted toward the end of my active service here was an uneasy feeling among the employees that they should have a greater voice in what was being done in departmental activities and in actions taken affecting them. They had no written statement of their belonging. As a step in that direction I wrote and circulated a code of conduct among the service here, and it was widely distributed I was told all through the country.

It was entitled "The Civil Servant's Pledge of Faith and Service" and it was written as follows: "I have faith in my country and its institutions. I believe in the importance of my job and in the dignity of all public service. I count myself fortunate to live and work in a state where I may obtain public employment through competition fairly won and under a system which permits me to look forward to a career as a public employee and advancement through merit.

"I know that government is no better than the people who direct its affairs and do its work. I will be honest, loyal, and industrious in the work I have to do. I will be courteous in my relations with my superiors, my fellow workers, and the public. I will use public property entrusted to my care for the purposes intended and protect and conserve it as though it were my own.

"I will refrain from doing anything that will bring discredit upon the state as my employer or upon me as a civil servant. I will strive, through my acts and my work, to realize the purposes for which government is established and so merit the esteem and respect of the people."

So far as I know, this was the first effort to put into words what might be considered the attitude of the desirable and effective public employee. Since then, millions of hours and dollars have been devoted to codes of conduct in hundreds of organizations of all kinds. It is an interesting pastime to compare these. My code is yet used so far as I know in some parts of the nation.

Q. What was the state of the merit system in New Jersey at the end of the 4th decade?

A. The troubled times of this period had its effects, of course. We continued on the broad foundations built in the thirties. There were some changes in the laws and the powers of the chairman of the commission were extended. Before he had gotten fully informed, he was persuaded to give up the checking of payrolls before payment. This was a troublesome and exacting role to be sure, but it is the one way to assure control of unauthorized appointments.

Q. I note that a great many new jurisdictions seemed to come in at one time. How did you handle so many at one time?

A. The fact of the matter was there was not enough employees to make much difference. We managed to get the new jurisdictions "on stream," as industry would say.

Q. Were labor-management relations difficult?

A. Not usually so. Employees were getting bolder, and more so-called leaders were beginning to talk about their rights. To my mind they have gone much too far and beyond their proper place, but maybe that is because I'm growing old.

Q. Were there any strikes?

A. Yes. I do not recall the exact date — probably in the early 40's when a laboring group in Newark, including the waste collectors, struck. The city authorities stood firm. There were charges and countercharges. Appeals were made to the Civil Service Commission. It stood firm, and said that employees would not be supported; get back to work, or get out. It became my task to write the decision. It could be said, I guess, that that decision became a sort of classic, in the country, for several years.

Q. I believe we have not discussed merit rating of employees. Did you have merit ratings in New Jersey?

A. Yes. Early in my time we had merit ratings forms as a part of promotion examinations. J. B. Probst, the Secretary and Examiner of the city of St. Paul, devised a complicated plan of merit rating. It was printed in pamphlet form in the thirties, and I wrote the foreword for the pamphlet. Mr. Probst had something. He made the mistake of throwing an air of mystery about it. His plan involved the keeping of the rating key himself. Had he not insisted on what looked like secrecy, I think his plan would have represented a constructive move toward this important but difficult problem in recording relative values of employees.

Q. What were the Princeton Surveys?

A. In the later 20's, Mr. Frank D. Schroth, the Assistant Publisher of the Times Newspapers, suggested that Professor Harold Dodds, whose long-time interest in public affairs had been known, make a study of the Trenton government. This was followed later by a study of Mercer County government. By reason of some happenings in some of the state departments, there developed a feeling that a study should be made of the state government. I was asked by some of the legislators what I thought about it and whom would I suggest to do the job. I indicated my favor of the proposal and suggested Dr. Dodds. He, assisted by a number of Princeton's younger men, undertook the task and made our office their state headquarters. Some improper practices were discovered and a few people lost their jobs. The study, however, had a wholesome effect. After Dr. Dodds had been made president of Princeton, on his own account and by reason of his continuing interest in public affairs, he set up the Princeton Surveys as a permanent organization to study government at state and local levels. He was particularly fortunate in getting Dr. John Sly as Director. I knew Dr. Sly first from our earlier associations at the Institute of Government at the University of Virginia. I kept in close touch with the Surveys as long as they existed. They performed a useful service.

Q. What was the effect of the Second World War?

A. About as distressing and upsetting as the first. It is hardly necessary to say that state and local government cannot operate normally in war times.

Q. What was the effect of the new constitution on the merit system?

A. I was getting ready to retire, so I avoided that project. I do not hesitate to say it was a decided improvement in many parts of the public service. It weakened, rather than strengthened, the merit system procedures.

Q. The enactment of legislation raising the Chairman — the President of the Commission — and clothing him with extensive powers was regarded as a very important piece of legislation. Why?

A. I believe that I should turn that question back to you. What do you think of it? You have in your hands wide executive and administrative powers. You are no longer subject to the commission ruling or decision; as I have said earlier, you are the agent of the Governor. While I was in service, those powers were not wisely handled.

Q. Dr. Messick, are you a specialist or a generalist?

A. I am not much on labels. I guess I am both. At least I have long been charged with that distinction.

Q. I have been going into the records. I find your fingerprints in a great many places in New Jersey and elsewhere. Back in 1922, you were President of the Civil Service Assembly; you were acting as a consultant to legislative committees and commissions; you were writing state papers of all kinds; you were somewhere, and usually in the vanguard, in every important city or state movement; you took over the records of the Civil Service Assembly after the Black Monday of '29, and became its president for three more years. When your Bureau had to close down, you were a member of all kinds of organizations related to governmental procedures; you were chairman of the Planning Board; you were chairman of the Board of Tourist Development; you were an educator of note and lectured throughout the country; you were a banker, a farmer, and other things; and you have not mentioned the fact that you served as executive assistant to the Governors. How did you do it? And I should add you stood out in all of these activities to one governor after another, and wrote his speeches, messages and did many other things for them.

A. Well, the record shows many of these things. You are responsible for the compliments. I thank you. I can say only I was always at it. I did what I could.

Q. Where did you get your training for all this?

A. Everywhere. I went to a little one-room country school with one teacher who was trained in a similar little school. I took county examinations for a teacher's certificate required then. When I was sixteen, I taught or kept a similar school to get enough money to start college. There were ten children in our family, and everyone of us followed the same course and taught school at one time or another. My father and mother were always telling us that we should get all the education we could because they did not want us to work as hard as they had to do. I guess I have worked harder than either of them. I'm still around. I never went to high school. The first day I ever spent in a high school was as a teacher. I came out with a pretty good record in college. I was chairman of the student body, the top officer in command of what we would now call the ROTC, captain of the football team, and president of my class, which office I yet hold.

We had a depression in 1907 and jobs were hard to come by. Our best engineering graduates felt themselves lucky to get $15 per week.

I was awarded a master's degree at Delaware in 1909, a master's at the University of Pennsylvania in 1911, an honorary Doctor of Laws by Delaware in 1933, an honorary Doctor of Business Administration by Rutgers in '34 and an honorary Doctor of Literature by Riders in 1946. In 1917, when I was promoted to the executive job in the Civil Service, I had 21 out of the 24 counts at Penn for the Ph. D., had selected the subject of my doctoral dissertation and collected most of the data upon which it was to be based. With all the things I was trying to do at the time, something had to give. The first thing was to discontinue my graduate school work.

Q. What do you consider your most noteworthy accomplishment?

A. I think it is fair to say that I fixed the place and the part of the personnel system in government, the proper place and the authority of its director, and demonstrated the truth of my convictions about the whole personnel system.

Q. What in your judgment is the value of this added Public Employment Commission relations where it may negotiate with public employees about the rights of the Civil Service Department?

A. I think it is an unwarranted and dangerous intervention. It should never have been enacted and the sooner that statute is repealed the better it will be for all parties concerned.

Q. Dr. Messick, do you have in mind one best precise form of personnel administration and no other that should be established?

A. No. I suppose I have shocked some people in the past by seeming impatient at their perfectionist attitude. I have said many times over the years, don't bother about these little things. Our present laws are better than our best possible administration of them. Until you are doing everything the law permits you to do, and doing it well, don't cry about what you can't do. Alexander Pope said two hundred and fifty years ago, "Of forms of government let fools contest, what'ere is best administered is best." Thousands of people in thousands of ways in a thousand books have been trying to say that in better ways. None of them has succeeded. For my part, I would eliminate the Civil Service Commission. I would place the public personnel system under a director with cabinet level, and require him to do the job.

Q. And what of the future?

A. I am hopeful, but I am not too confident. I have little sympathy with the foolish youngsters, particularly those whose parents gave them everything that they wanted and more, and who now pay them back by wandering around in rags and filth, defying all sanitary and moral standards and talking about a generation gap.

To be sure, parents of this generation must carry some of the blame. Discipline should have been the word instead of indulgence. But these children will be our leaders tomorrow. They will set the standards and raise their children. Too many of them I'm afraid have gathered scars in their silly and dangerous actions in pursuit of what they call their new freedom and defiance that will trouble them for life. We have lost a great deal in the strength and majesty of our country. It will take us a long time to get back to the standards that have been our pride and distinction.

Our task here in New Jersey is to recapture some of that old dedication and concern for better public administration and seek to get back to these old standards. The problems and their solutions belong to you and those who follow.

* * * * *

Druz: I would like to continue this conversation, but I must stop somewhere and, perhaps, this is the proper place. I have followed the work of Dr. Messick from almost his beginning. I am proud to have been a part of it, and when I came into the Department of the Civil Service, as I have said above, I was trained by him. Several of his secretarial staff were yet in the department. I kept hearing these older employees saying many times in those earlier days Dr. Messick would say this or that should be done. I have learned many of the reasons they said these things. My task, I'm sure, our task, is not to seek new ways, but to get back to doing things the way they were done back there when the personnel work here was the model for all to follow.

I am greatly pleased and impressed by what I have heard in these sessions. Here is the man, old in years, he is ninety years old, he has the same keen and active mind that he had when he was making history here and in the nation. The fact remains that he made a great contribution to this state and to all America. He was not always free from attack, but he plowed straight through it all to the goal that he saw. His way, after all, was brightened by commendation and praise. Whether the times create the leader or the leader creates the times, no one knows. We do know that this state was fortunate in having this type of leadership in New Jersey. We say again that no man has done more in the art of public administration in his generation than he.

* * * * *

Q. Dr. Messick in closing this interesting discussion will you give us a parting summary of what you see ahead and your thoughts for the future?

A. I am afraid that what I may say further would be merely repetition. In this extended discussion we have covered, it seems to me, much of the basic material that may well be included for the purposes intended. It can be said that many things and conditions can change our emphasis by reason of the changing times. In times of war we make no progress in advancing the methods of government; this is a peacetime effort.

As we discuss these matters today, many people do not want to enter the public service. The time will come again when many people will seek public service employment. Assurance of employment, higher pay, and greater fringe benefits, will bring this about. What we should be concerned about is industrious, devoted, public employees whose work is reflected in better government, at less expense, relatively, because we cannot live in the old political, grasping, way and remain the great and strong nation we want to be and must be, as the example to the world of a democracy with all its freedoms and individual opportunity. Vigilance and not neglect will assure this. Our ways of government must be improved if we are to live in the long future. Good personnel, fairly treated, properly organized and directed, properly paid, and where all shall work for the state and none for self, is the answer.

We are preparing to celebrate our nation's two hundredth anniversary. The wrecks of empires strewn along the path of history are a forceable reminder of their death, and none of them lived for two hundred years. We should not forget the words of Ben Franklin when he said to the Continental Congress "You now have a government if you can keep it." He was saying that we could lose that government by neglect, from the inside, not by conquest by an outside enemy. Our aim, our safety, and our very existence will depend on what we do within our government. We must think on these things.

Q. As I have been asking you all these questions, I have been wondering how you stood up under the immense burdens you were carrying, even though I was there and saw you doing it. I just said I would not ask another question, but I feel that I must. What was deep inside, which you had not told anyone, that drove you on?

A. I will try to answer that question. It was, perhaps, a number of things — not vanity, or money, or publicity. It was I believe an innate desire to leave something that would help somebody who might feel that I had helped and that he might be able to say: "I am better because he passed this way."

* * * * *

Druz: I see! The greatest compliment I can pay to you is that you were always right in your convictions, and say further that I am the first to say that to you, and that what you have said today will be my guiding light in all I try to do in following your example. I know that what we have recorded here will be the aim of many others as the years pass. You have been a faithful servant, in your community, your state, and your country.

CHAPTER 10

Renewal and Recovery

We are told that man is born to trouble as the smoke flies upward, and history records it. There is always trouble and disaster somewhere, and in the many places where these conditions occur, the population becomes discouraged and comes to the belief that they are everywhere, that they have come to stay.

Our America is passing through one of these difficult periods. We here in the United States are paying the price of our waste and neglect, of carelessness and indifference, of danger and disaster. Wars and rumors of wars are all about us; the Far East is a tinder box; South America is a close second; poverty and unemployment are everywhere; and crime walks our streets boldly and unafraid. We no longer trust each other or our government, little and big, from the hamlet to Washington. We hear a lone voice now and then for calm consideration and common sense, but for the most part we see partners and individuals playing the political game and ignoring the needs of the people. We see attacks on big business and little business, on wealth and poverty, argument and speeches, laws and investigations, but little constructive action.

There is a way, or rather there are ways out of this disaster. We have had serious problems before and have come through successfully, picked up the controls we had dropped and moved on in our course to greater things, and we can and will do this again but it will require calmness and common sense.

Recently the Chase Manhattan National Bank, even though it along with other banks of the country have had and are having their own troubles, carried a full-page advertisement in the *Wall Street Journal* giving a plan of recovery that contains common sense and reason, and is free from political considerations. Yet thus far there has been no record, editorial or otherwise, from a rather careful scrutiny of the daily press carrying the news of Washington and the neighboring area, of any member of Congress mentioning or commenting on that advertisement. I quote, with the permission of Chase:

> What if we told you one out of six American workers would be out of a job ten years from now?
>
> Possibly you.
>
> Not because you couldn't or didn't want to work, but because American industry would be starved for capital.
>
> There would be no tools for you to work with, no materials to work on.
>
> You squawk. And scream. Get fighting mad. And do something.
>
> Well, if we go along the way we have been, Chase foresees a massive capital shortfall by 1985.
>
> With consequent high levels of unemployment. Levels double what we have now.
>
> During the next 10 years the country must find enough capital to control pollution. Provide sufficient housing. Finance our federal budget. Become independent in energy. Improve mass transit.
>
> American industry must also find enough money to buy the machinery and tools — the capital plant needed to deliver jobs for everybody who wants one.
>
> Our economists believe there won't be enough money for both.

The shortfall could reach $1.5 trillion. Or $400 million a day every day for the next 10 years.

Failure to close this capital gap will result in significantly higher unemployment and a higher inflation rate 10 years from now. Both unacceptable conditions.

As a sensible, long-term solution, Chase proposes that thought be given to a seven-point action program:

- Encourage an ever-growing base of personal savings.
- Establish more realistic depreciation allowances.
- Give preferential tax treatment for retained corporate earnings re-invested in the business.
- Ease our harsh treatment of capital gains compared with that of most other countries.
- Stabilize fiscal and monetary policy to prevent violent swings in the economy.
- Encourage foreign investment in the U. S. economy.
- Eliminate unnecessary controls, and outmoded government regulations.

Impossible? We should try it or prepare and institute a better plan. At any rate we should quit playing kings in the corner and getting nowhere.

CHAPTER 11

Light Your Own Fire

In my lifetime I have tried to do or to get others to do many things that I believed to be for the public good. Sometimes I have succeeded and at other times I have failed. I have had my share of commendations and my share of criticism. I have expected that and I do not complain.

I am not a genius. I do not want to be one. In my long and varied career I have faced many problems having to do with many situations and the well-being of many people. In all of these cases or things, I first ask myself what is the right answer for me to give or make, not because I am more honest or more concerned than other people. I want to be right and to give the best answer that I can. I have found that I can sleep better with myself that way and that I can last longer as a friend and advisor.

I have met some people who think and respond as I do, and I have met others who think I am naive and old fashioned. Be that as it is or may be, I am willing to stand or fall on my own decisions. I have met geniuses. I do not wish to be numbered among them. I have found in most instances that they are as persistent in their thinking as I am in mine, that they believe in matters that are the opposite of my own beliefs. And many of them, perhaps most of them, act and talk quite differently from the way I see things or talk about them. I met Albert Einstein once. He was a genius, real and in the flesh. He proved it by his discoveries and their possible application, but he paid the price. His recreations were different from those about him; so far as is known he could not see the beauty of a rainbow, the flowers in the meadow or the starry skies. He lived alone in this great and beautiful world of ours. Seemingly he could not talk as neighbors and friends talk. When he sought surcease from his thoughts, he walked down the railroad tracks stepping from tie to tie. He was obliged, it was said that he never went out alone, but had a companion following near lest he got lost, get confused, and be unable to find his way back to his home or wherever he might be staying. When he shook hands his hand was cold; It had no friendly pressure, no warmth; yet he was great. He was a genius, capable of great thoughts that made the world wonder. He paid the price for his talents.

Sometime ago I heard a thinking man say that a strong man, one who makes his mark and gets worthwhile things done, must have drive and persistence to light his own fire. That phrase stayed with me, and I saw, or thought I saw, something of my own drive and persistence in getting things done that seemed to me necessary and desirable over my long years of public service. I, too, was always pressing against the wind. I was trying to light my own fire.

Many people have asked me and some even yet ask me, what they should do or what their children should do in the selection of their life's work and what is the best way to prepare for that work? Not in the same words, but what I said to these concerned people was along the same lines of what this wise observer said, "light your own fire." This quality is the most important quality every father and mother, every puzzled young man and woman asks himself and herself and others. It is a part of them, as close as their heart beat. Those who follow this course, earnestly and sincerely will find success in their work, peace of mind, joy in living and the guidelines and landmarks clear and sure as he presses on toward his own goals. "Light Your Own Fire!"

CHAPTER 12

Epilogue to One Man's Life

The following untitled poem was recently sent me by a friend who wrote: "I never knew anybody to whom this was more applicable. It would almost seem that this author even then (in 1929) must have known and foreseen your career."

Lord, let me die, working.
Still tackling plans unfinished, tasks undone.
Clean to its end, swift may my race be run.
No laggard steps, no faltering, no shirking.
Lord, let me die, working.

Lord, let me die, thinking.
Let me fare forth still with an open mind.
Fresh secrets to unfold, new truths to find.
My soul undimmed, alert, no questions blinking.
Lord, let me die, thinking.

Lord, let me die, laughing.
No sighing o'er past sins; they are forgiven.
Spilled on this earth are all the joys of heaven;
The wine of life, the cup of mirth quaffing.
Lord, let me die, laughing.

Dr. S. Hall Young
(September 2, 1927)